# Praise for *Lightwo*

"Do you want to know your soul purpose? Are you ready to fulfil your spiritual potential? Then George Lizos's new book is a must. It is filled with practical tips and exercises as it takes you on a journey of deep connection to who you really are and why you are here. I loved it."

**Diana Cooper, bestselling author of *The Archangel Guide to Ascension***

"Let George take you on a transformational journey to discover your life's purpose. This book will help you to understand your true lightworker abilities and how to make an impact through your work. Authentic, inspirational and practical, this book has all your lightworker needs covered!"

**Emma Mumford, author of *Spiritual Queen* and *Positively Wealthy***

"George Lizos is a powerful and unique spiritual teacher, who comes directly from the heart. He is to be cherished!"

**Yasmin Boland, international astrologer and bestselling author of *Moonology***

"In the noisy landscape of self-help influencers, George Lizos's clear, bright voice stands out. George's message of hope and healing feels so true, not only because he communicates the timeless wisdom of the heavens, but also because he is grounded so deeply in his own truth down here on earth."

**Jordan Bach, author and life coach**

"George's fresh take on how we can work our light and live our best life now is the positive nudge we need to evolve as one balanced, and harmonious human tribe."

**Calista, author of *Unicorn Rising* and *The Female Archangels***

"*Lightworkers Gotta Work* is one of the most practical spiritual books I've ever read. George is a modern-day renaissance man who helps you navigate your spiritual journey no matter what sex you are. This book is a must read for anyone seeking more direction in their life and ultimately connecting more to their purpose. Through the chapters, George creates a step-by-step framework for you to practice and embody his teachings, which will help you accept and love yourself on all levels. Thank you, George for putting your work into the world so that it can be a better place – you are a true lightworker through and through."

**Danielle Paige, intuitive astrologer and spiritual teacher**

"*Lightworkers Gotta Work* is a must read for anyone who has that niggling feeling that they are here to help this planet in a big way, but hasn't quite worked out how. This book is filled to overflowing with activities, tips and tricks to help the reader boost their intuitive connection, balance their masculine and feminine energies, work with energy, and move through just about anything that may come up on the spiritual pathway. If you know you have a light within you but need a hand turning it on, activating it and sharing it with the world, this book needs to be on your shelf, by your bed, or in your bag at all times!"

**Victoria "Vix" Maxwell, intuitive and author of *Class of 1983***

"In *Lightworkers Gotta Work*, George Lizos leads the reader on a journey of lightwork, through his compelling personal stories that are in service to the work, and step-by-step levels of tools and mastery. In inclusive, direct, and progressive spiritual analysis, George lifts high-minded spiritual seeking from dogma, anti-intellectualism, and outdated beliefs on sexuality and gender. If you do the work in *Lightworkers Gotta Work*, you'll find yourself walking a path with George as a friend and the Universe as a guide. I highly recommend it for anyone looking for a way in, a mentor, and/or a refresher on the universal themes. Thank you, George, for putting in this work to help us all rise to your excellence!"

**Colin Bedell, astrologer and author of *Queer Cosmos***

# Lightworkers GOTTA WORK

The Ultimate Guide to Following Your
Purpose and Creating Change in the World

## GEORGE LIZOS

First published by That Guy's House, 2020
www.thatguyshouse.com

None of the information in this book should substitute professional medical advice; the reader is advised to always consult a medical practitioner. The use of any information in this book is at the reader's risk and discretion, and the author cannot be held liable for its misuse.

That Guy's House

# CONTENTS

*The world won't change sitting in meditation pillows all day long.*

# FORWARD

Who is the good guy?

You see, in every story throughout time, there has been a good guy and a bad guy: David and Goliath, the hero vs. the villain, light vs. darkness, masculine vs. feminine. While turning the pages of mythology, folklore and even the nursery rhymes that sent us off to sleep as children, we're always cheering on a winner and denouncing a loser. These tropes are embedded in our collective storyline, engrained in us and etched into our souls.

Today, in an evolving world where certain words are now outdated and offensive, we find ourselves needing to change the narrative accordingly. We are seeing job tittles become gender neutral, as salesman becomes sales person or sales rep, anchorman becomes anchor and chairman become a chair, which leads me to ask if the term 'bad guy' is also outdated? Can only men be bad? Can only masculine energy be bad? Is it time that we evolved our narrative and our attitude to become gender- and energy-balanced, too?

I am a big believer in personal evolution. As a writer with spiritual liberation at the core of my words, I have studied and scribed thousands of words on exploring the soul and the self on one's own terms, digging into the underbelly of true energy and purpose. One thing that has blown me away when crossing paths with people on this journey to self-expansion is that there are many who aren't looking at their self from all angles; their *whole* self. Instead, they work only on one side of their energy, rather than acknowledging and experiencing all of their converging facets: the light and the dark, Yin and Yang, good and bad, masculine and feminine. If you are learning about yourself and your divine energy, there is no point only learning half of it. After all, you don't just makeover half of your hair, or workout one arm and neglect the other, unless you want one Popeye arm and a hell of a hairdo. The same rule applies to working with the soul; two halves make a whole.

On occasions where you meet someone who is working with both their halves in balance, you immediately identify their openness to complementary energies, as their feminine and masculine greet you in unison. One of the most powerful people I have worked with in this space is the author of this book, George Lizos. Luckily for you, you've also met him after picking up this book and letting his balanced energy wrap around you from within its pages. Trust me, you'll feel a different energy in these words, as his approach will speak to you on a new level. It's nurturing yet impactful, and powerfully aligned.

By letting him be your guide, you will evolve through the experience of reading his work. He will nudge awake parts of your soul's energy, and, as is usually the case when we first awaken to something, you may feel bright-eyed and energized by spiritual truth, or perhaps even a tad agitated and grouchy – both are OK. Allow the half of you which has been hibernating to stir in its own time, as you explore how to awaken, warm up and work with the energy of your whole divine self.

**Emma Mildon**

Bestselling author of *The Soul Searcher's Handbook* and *Evolution of Goddess*

# INTRODUCTION

I see you, lightworker. You care about this world. You care about other people. You have a deep yearning, an insatiable desire to help others heal and our planet thrive. In fact, you've felt this way ever since you were a little child. You stood out from the crowd like a unicorn in a herd of horses. You were more sensitive than other kids your age. You perceived the world, and people, in different ways.

You may not have known it then, but you definitely felt it; that you came to this world to fulfil a purpose bigger than yourself and beyond your own personal wellbeing. Of course, you knew then and you certainly know now that you deserve to live a joyful, abundant and purposeful life. However, the desire your soul desperately yearns for goes beyond the personal sphere to encompass the collective wellbeing and ascension of the world.

Your soul's yearning is so strong because it's rooted in hundreds, if not thousands, of incarnations of trials and tribulations, wins and losses, highs and lows, all culminating in this present lifetime where you get to finally make it.

Lightworker, you're called to action!

You heard the call and thought that you'd answered it, but really, all you've done is scratch the surface of what you can do and who you can be. This is the lifetime where you get to actualise lifetimes' worth of dreams and desires. This is the lifetime where you get to find, follow and fulfil your life purpose of finding happiness, helping others heal and creating a big, positive change in the world. This is the lifetime where we work together to help in the ascension of the planet and the creating of the heaven on earth that we know we, and our planet, deserve.

The world doesn't change sitting in meditation pillows all day long. The world changes when lightworkers like you and me light up and get to work. This book will help you do just that.

## Your Lightworker Journey

Before you get started on your lightworker journey to following and fulfilling your life purpose, it's important to identify where you currently are on that journey. From my experience in working with lightworkers over many years, you probably fall into one of the following two categories:

1. **You don't know what your *specific* life purpose is.** Instead, you're familiar with our *collective* lightworker purpose of helping people heal and making a positive change in the world.

2. **You know your life purpose, but you're held back by fears and limiting beliefs that keep you stuck.** As a result, you don't take consistent action towards your purpose, or you tend to over-depend on the Universe for support.

Whichever of these two statements is true for you, I want to assure you that by the end of this book, you'll have the clarity you need to take forward action. You'll have a clear definition of your life purpose, and you'll have equipped yourself with practical and powerful spiritual tools to follow and fulfil it.

I know how it feels, lightworker. I've been there myself, not so long ago. I lacked clarity and was catapulted by fears and limiting beliefs that prevented me from accepting my authenticity and following my purpose. I kept my spirituality in the closet for fear of what others might think, suppressed my dreams thinking I'd never be good enough to follow them, and opted for living a conventional, soul-draining life that rid me of my joy and creativity.

The processes I share in this book are the exact processes I've used, and still use, to effectively own and work my light. The path I'll guide you through has helped me to accept my worthiness, embrace my spirituality in all its woo-ness and fearlessly follow my purpose. It's my hope and promise that by the end of this book, you'll be on your way to doing the same.

## How to Read This Book

*Lightworkers Gotta Work* is not an inspirational book. Inspiration gratifies you for a while, but then it dissipates and you're off searching for the next ephemeral fix. Instead, the purpose of this book is spiritual transformation. It's packed with practical processes that'll help you know and embody the concepts and practices in a deep and palpable way. If you do the work and follow the processes, you'll be a different person by the end of it.

The book is divided into four parts that build on one another to equip you with all the tools you need to find, follow and fulfil your life purpose:

Part I – **Find Your Purpose** explores the concept of the life purpose, guiding you towards finding and defining it in a specific, two-paragraph definition.

Part II – **Nurture Your Light** focuses on awakening feminine energy. It introduces a variety of techniques, tips and processes to help you deepen your alignment with your inner being.

Part III – **Work Your Light** is about expressing masculine energy. It delves into advanced manifestation processes to help you receive intuitive guidance and co-create with the Universe in following your life purpose.

Part IV – **Protect Your Light** explores psychic tools and spiritual guidance to help you protect your sensitivity and guard the sacredness of your purpose on the way to fulfilling it.

I've written this book mindfully to guide you through the specific steps you need to take in order to find and follow your life purpose. Although you may be guided to read the book in a different order than it's written, my advice is that you read it sequentially. I've written each chapter to follow and build on the previous one, so reading it from start to finish will ensure you get maximum benefit from it.

Since this is a practical book, on many occasions I'll ask you to take pen and paper and write things down. As a result, it'll be beneficial to have a journal dedicated to this journey. Whether it is an electronic or a physical one, keeping all the processes in one place will help you to keep track of your progress and revisit the practices when you need to.

## We're in This Together

I'm fully committed to helping you get to the finish line, and I want to be there for you every step of the way. Here's what you can do to help me support you on this journey:

1. **Join my private Facebook Group community, *Your Spiritual Toolkit*.** This is a safe and supportive community of likeminded lightworkers, who are all on this journey with you. Use this group to ask questions, contribute with your answers and share your journey through the book. I'm actively involved in the group and I'll be there to cheer you on along the way.

2. **Follow me on Instagram (@georgelizos) and keep me posted on your progress.** Send me DMs and tag

me in your posts and stories using the hashtag #LightworkersGottaWork. I read all of my comments and messages and personally reply to everything.

3. **Download the *Lightworkers Gotta Work Checklist* at** GeorgeLizos.com/LGW. This includes a list of all the processes and meditations in the book, so you can tick them off as you complete them. It's a great way to keep yourself accountable on your journey.

I look forward to hearing from you and supporting you along your lightworker journey. I have every confidence in you, and I can't wait to see the magic you create in the world.

# A NOTE ON TERMS

## Lightworker

In her book *Light is The New Black*, Rebecca Campbell defines a lightworker as 'someone who wholeheartedly makes the decision to make the world a brighter place by being in it.' I also agree with this definition, and from this perspective every person in the world is a lightworker, provided that they consciously choose to make the world a brighter place.

That being said, although there are lightworkers in all walks of life, this book speaks directly to lightworkers within the spiritual community. *Lightworkers Gotta Work* is a call to action for spiritual seekers, teachers, healers, artists and entrepreneurs who wish to create change in the world through their spiritual work. When I refer to the term lightworker throughout the book, I speak directly to this group of spiritually-minded lightworkers, rather than the broader spectrum of lightworkers.

However, in making such categorisations it can become easy to fall into the trap of spiritual egotism, thinking that our group or collective purpose is more special or important than other people, groups and purposes, or that we're here to save others. This is not the case, nor is it the message of this book.

Be mindful of such tendencies arising, and keep reminding yourself that we (the entire world population) are all in this together. No group of lightworkers, or people for that matter, is more special or important than any other group of people in the world. We're all equally important in bringing upon the ascension and evolution of the planet.

## Masculine and Feminine Energy

Throughout the book, I talk about the Divine Feminine and Divine Masculine, as well as feminine and masculine energy in general. A question that usually arises when I teach about these terms in my workshops and courses is how they relate with terms such as sex, gender and sexuality.

Here's the distinction:

Sex is biological, i.e. male, female, other, etc.

Gender is social, i.e. man, woman, non-binary, etc.

Sexuality is biological, i.e. gay, straight, bisexual, etc.

The Divine Feminine and Divine Masculine are energies that are present in, and expressed through, all three arenas. While men tend to have more masculine energy and women tend to have more feminine energy, these energies are present within everyone irrespective of sex, gender or sexuality.

# PART I

# FIND YOUR PURPOSE

# Chapter 1

# LIT-STARVED TO LIT UP

I was a weird kid. I spent most of my time alone out in nature, staring up at the sky and pondering life's big questions. In fact, the fondest childhood memory I have is of me as a five-year-old George, standing in a field of yellow daisies wondering who I was, why I was here and what my life's purpose was. Looking back on my life now, that's when I first realised that I was a lightworker. As a child, I was in tune with my light. I felt it, I was it and I worked it, not consciously, but innately, like we all do.

We're all born knowing our own loveliness, perfectly balanced in our masculine and feminine energies, and having a clear, intuitive awareness of our life purpose. We're also born with a direct connection to Source, giving us moment-to-moment guidance as to when to take action (masculine) and when to surrender (feminine) in order to follow and fulfil that purpose.

As happens with most of us, when we grow up, we eventually get indoctrinated into a patriarchal world of rules, stereotypes, expectations and set formulas for success that subsequently disconnect us from our balance and inner guidance. We're taught that a masculine approach to life – hard work, struggle and eventually exhaustion – is the only approach, and that a feminine approach – resting, surrendering and trusting our intuition – is lazy and unproductive. For me, the disconnection from my light was probably deeper and more traumatic than it was for most people.

## Becoming The Guru

Growing up on the small, conservative, Mediterranean island of Cyprus meant that I also had to play it small and conservative. Sameness was glorified, and difference in all its forms was rejected. Spirituality had to be Christian-based, and little boys had to grow up to be strong, straight men – patriarchy in all its glory. And then there was shy, woo-woo, feminine me, feeling like an ugly duckling in a lake of perfectly sculptured swans.

*I have to fit in*, I'd tell myself, as this inner thought became an obsession in the early part of my life – an obsession that would eventually dim my light and almost extinguish it. Feeling like an outcast, I tried to be the perfect son for my parents, the perfect student at school and the perfect citizen in society. The ugly feminine duckling had to be suppressed. I had to be the strong, masculine swan I was expected to be, or I'd disappoint my family and the world.

So, I taught myself to be normal. I played football like all boys did, I performed well at school to get praised by my teachers and parents, and I even attempted to have friends other than the trees and flowers that I usually hung out with. I became good at it. I learned what people needed to see and hear to tick me off as normal on their list, and I gave it to them. The bullying and occasional punches I used to get from older brash boys at school ceased, for the most part, and I was winning in my quest to transform myself into the stereotype everyone wanted me to be.

This seemingly blissful period was only short-lived, though, as things were set to go awry once I realised that I was gay. I was thirteen years old at the time, and the only information I had about homosexuality was uttered in stifled whispers and came with a series of warnings. As far as I was concerned at that tender age, gay people were criminals and paedophiles who you had to stay away from. There were no gay role models on TV, and no one to go to for guidance. It became clear that adding the gay label to the series of ugly duckling labels that I'd already had put on me would destroy any chances I had of fitting in.

I had to take action, fast. Homosexuality had become my nemesis; it had to be obliterated. So, I did what I do best: I decided I'd take a practical, masculine approach and change myself from gay to straight one step at a time. That's when I entered the two most debilitating years of my life. Between my thirteenth and fifteenth years, I put myself through a mental, emotional and physical boot camp, as I tried to change my sexuality. I monitored the way I walked, the way I talked, my mannerisms and my hand gestures. I censored gay thoughts from my mind, suppressed my emotions and even forced myself to fantasise about women. I *had* to be straight.

I wasn't, though, and there was no way for me to change who I was born to be. Two years of failed attempts to turn me straight later, I decided that I was a human abomination who would never be able to make it in life. I saw only one way out, and it was by doing everyone a favour and taking myself out of the game once and for all.

In what will always stay in my mind as a dark and cold night, I found myself crying in my room, tortured by my life's failures. My eyes stung with tears as I picked up a piece of paper and a pen and started scribbling down: *I'm sorry for what I did. I just can't live with myself anymore… this way. I've tried to change, but I can't. I want you to know that I love you and I'm sorry.* Then, I gently let the pen down and picked up the small plastic box I had stolen from the first-aid kit moments before, pulling out the pill case and coming face-to-face with my future. I popped a few pills out and hesitantly threw them into my mouth. I felt empty and liberated at the same time, as I took the glass of water from my desk and took a large sip.

Thankfully, I didn't take the rest of the pills. In that moment of surrender, the light I'd suppressed came flooding back into my body and soul, giving me the solution that had always been available to me, but which I had resisted for so long. At that moment, I realised I did have a choice. I could simply say fuck what other people think about me and learn to love and accept myself exactly as I am, and that's what I did.

From that moment on, I made the commitment to embrace the feminine side of myself, loving and accepting both my sexuality and me fully, along with all my differences and intricacies. I didn't know how, but it didn't matter because I was willing to learn how to do so. I was lit up once again; the purity and connectedness I had as a five-year-old reignited within me, and I launched myself on a path of healing and transformation.

Louise Hay's *You Can Heal Your Life* was one of the first books that popped up, helping me as it did to forgive my bullies, and myself, and teaching me practical steps towards loving my body and my sexuality. From that, I went on to study a variety of spiritual modalities and traditions, each one helping me release the past and come back to my power. Five years of spiritual growth later, I was finally free from the struggles of my past, standing proudly in my light and ready to help others do the same. I was inspired to write my first book, *Be the Guru: A Step-by-Step Guide to Becoming Your Own Spiritual Teacher*, detailing the process I used to liberate myself from other people's control while learning to find all the happiness, support and wisdom I needed within myself.

It felt as if my spiritual path had reached a level of maturity. I was healed and empowered; I'd overcome the wrath of patriarchy, embraced my feminine energy and taught others to do the same. I was working my light, not just being it. Little did I know, however, that the control of patriarchy was more deep-seated than I expected. Although I had made strides in peeling off a thick layer of patriarchy that had me rejecting, and even trying to destroy, my femininity for good, it was merely one layer. My path to embracing the Divine Feminine fully, and eventually finding balance between masculine and feminine energy, was only just beginning.

## The Patriarchy Trap

Until that moment, my approach to life and work before and after my spiritual transformation hadn't changed at all: it was purely masculine. I believed in making detailed plans, working hard on them and taking action to the point of exhaustion. I willingly and proudly sacrificed sleep, potential romantic relationships and my social life, all for the purpose of hustling hard for my dreams and desires. On the other hand, I looked down on people who spent time relaxing, taking it easy and having fun. Deep down, I was still a victim of the masculine approach to life that I'd been indoctrinated into in my early years growing up in Cyprus.

By my mid-twenties, I'd graduated with bachelor's and master's degrees in the UK, and had started working for a popular Mind–Body–Spirit publishing house in London. It was a way for me to give back to the authors whose work had saved my life early on, but also a great opportunity for me to support myself financially while developing my own spiritual business. It was a great plan, and I was thrilled to be able to give back while also doing my own thing. Little did I know that these three years of my life would be responsible for leading me to my next big spiritual transformation, and for helping me finally find the balance I'd been missing.

My daily schedule went something like this: I'd wake up at seven in the morning, work a nine-to-five job, come home from work and start working on my own business until midnight, and then repeat the following day. My weekends were also dedicated to working on my business, which meant that I had to isolate myself from friends, abstain from all sorts of social and romantic pursuits, and be a monster of action and productivity. Patriarchy might have failed at killing me off during my teenage years, but it was certainly succeeding in my twenties.

I first realised that my obsessive, unbalanced work life was an issue when I woke up one morning intending to go to work, but my body just wouldn't function. I'd literally exhausted myself to the point that my muscles were refusing to move. Although it became obvious that my approach was unhealthy, I ignored my own guidance and kept at it. I almost felt proud of exhausting myself, as if I'd finally become the superhuman I always knew lived within me. This would surely prove to all the kids and people who rejected me in my childhood that I wasn't just another swan like them, but that I was in fact the strongest, most beautiful swan of all.

Here's the thing about patriarchy. Having dominated our society for almost six thousand years, it's so deeply rooted in the fabric of life, our work culture and our spirituality that even when we believe we've escaped it, we're still victims of it. If you take the analogy of patriarchy being a city and you being a prisoner within a house in that city, escaping the house feels like freedom from the city, whereas you're actually still within it. The good news is that the first house you escape from shows you what's out there; it introduces you to a whole new world of opportunities that are healthier, happier and more fulfilling, and you crave for more. Then, the next time you escape, you find yourself in a shady neighbourhood, and you don't take freedom for granted anymore. You look for more ways to escape.

I was in a shady neighbourhood having overworked myself, but it wasn't until after a couple more similar instances of exhaustion that I decided to do something about it. By my third year working a full-time job while running my business part-time, I'd realised that my lifestyle wasn't sustainable. I'd become this robotic, detached person who worked a lot and lived a little. My friendships suffered, my love life was non-existent, my health was deteriorating, and I was even feeling stagnant and disconnected in my spirituality.

## Finding the Goddess in Avalon

I knew I had to take action, and I knew it had to be in Glastonbury, UK. Glastonbury had been my escape from the city, a place for me to relax and recalibrate, throughout the seven years I'd lived in the UK. Thought to have been the ancient city of Avalon, and the final home of King Arthur himself, Glastonbury is a quaint little town in the southwest of England that marks the central point of many spiritual paths and religions. Christians revere it as the place where Joseph of Arimathea had allegedly hidden the Holy Grail following Jesus's resurrection, and the New Age and spiritual communities at large consider it to be one of few points on our planet where the Divine Masculine and Divine Feminine energies merge in perfect balance.

Two of the world's most dominant ley lines, the Mary and the Michael – one representing the Divine Feminine, and the other the Divine Masculine – cross at the Chalice Well Gardens at the foot of the famous Glastonbury Tor. From the Tor flow two streams of water, the red spring and the white spring. The red, iron-infused spring has a subtle reddish colour and represents the Divine Feminine, flowing into the Chalice Well, a well within a beautiful faery garden at the foot of the Tor. The white, calcium-infused spring has a paler colour and represents the Divine Masculine. The white spring flows through the Tor and into the White Spring Cave right next to the Chalice Well. As they merge, they energetically and symbolically mark the balance of feminine and masculine energy.

What's interesting is that in the seven years I'd been visiting Glastonbury, I was never able to find the White Spring Cave. I knew it existed, I was well aware of the story behind it, and yet every time I went out looking for it, I'd end up in the Chalice Well garden instead, bathing in the Divine Feminine energy of the red spring. It was as if my entire being was fed up of the masculine energy of the city, and longed for the feminine energy that overflowed from the gardens.

This time, Source had a different plan for me. Although my being still craved feminine energy, I somehow knew that I had to search for and find it within the masculine. It didn't make much sense to me at the time, but it felt right, and I had to trust my gut.

Without even actively searching for it, on my first morning out in the town I found myself in the entrance of the White Spring Cave. As I walked in, I was taken aback not just by the beauty and the sacredness of it, but also by people's reverence and dedication to it. The candle-lit cave was adorned with three altars: one to Brigid, Celtic Fire Goddess; one to Cernunnos, the King of the Faeries; and the final and central one to the spirit of the White Spring. Set-up just behind a series of giant pools of water flowing from the White Spring at the back of the cave, people would take off their clothes, lay out their offerings and baptise themselves in the pool.

Walking into the cave, I felt as if I'd let go of a breath that I hadn't known I'd been holding in. It felt as if I'd finally returned home after years of forcefully being kept away from it, and after splashing some water on my face, instilling in me the masculine energy I'd been at war with my entire life, I sat and meditated in a corner of the cave for what could have been hours. Coming out of the meditation, I knew exactly what I was supposed to do. As if in a trance, I walked out of the cave and booked an appointment for a past life regression with Atasha Fyfe, author of *Magical Past Lives*.

This regression would change my life. The past life I regressed to was similar to a series of past lives I'd experienced in previous regressions. For the three years I'd been stuck in my unbalanced, masculine lifestyle, each time I'd regress to a past life I'd get the same story repeated with just a different set of characters, countries and times.

In these past lives, I'm always a prostitute choosing to suppress my emotions and objectify my femininity, and the past life that Atasha regressed me to was the source of it all. It was the lifetime that created a trauma big enough for me to not just reject the Divine Feminine in that lifetime, but to reject it in the lives that followed as well.

In the regression, I saw myself getting pregnant by one of my clients. When I told him what had happened, he took a sharp knife and planted it deep into my womb, killing the baby and leaving me scarred for life. In that lifetime, as my femininity was literally torn away from me, I vowed to reject and keep rejecting it. As a result, lifetime after lifetime I relived the same pattern of rejecting my femininity and abusing my masculinity in one way or another. In my current lifetime, my feminine energy expressed itself in the form of my homosexuality, which I also tried to destroy, and although I'd thankfully aborted my one attempt at suicide, I was still destroying it slowly with my unsustainable masculine way of life.

I left my session with Atasha with a clear goal in mind. I had to embrace the Divine Feminine more in my life. Until that point, although I was consciously connecting to Source and was deeply devoted to my spiritual path, I wasn't consciously honouring the feminine aspect of Source. Growing up as an Orthodox Christian, I was taught that God was male, and even though I'd come to the realisation later on in my spiritual path that there are both masculine and feminine aspects to Source, my default was to think of, and honour, Source as being masculine.

The regression made it clear to me that consciously honouring the masculine and feminine sides of Source was the key to finding balance, not just in my spirituality, but in every part of my life. The people we are in our everyday lives, along with our interests, personalities and life purpose, all draw from our soul. Our soul is the spiritual side of our physical heart, and is therefore responsible for managing the relationship between our physicality and our spirituality. It sends information through from Source, informing our physicality of the guidance we need to follow to be fully authentic, find balance in masculine and feminine energy, and move forward with our life purpose.

There are many ways we can disconnect from our soul (at least partially, for we can never fully disconnect from it); some are ephemeral and some are long-standing. In my experience, the harshest way to disconnect from our soul, and the toughest to mend, is to not know our soul for what it really is. Thinking we know our soul when we don't changes our perception of ourselves and the world, and sends us down a path of slow and painful destruction, a path where happiness and fulfilment can only be experienced partially, but never fully.

Since our soul is a droplet of Source itself within a physical body, not knowing our soul means that we don't know Source, and thus the way we lead ourselves in the world is disconnected from Source. In my case, I didn't know my soul, and therefore Source, for what they fully were. I only knew one side of them – the masculine side. Seeing only the Divine Masculine side of Source meant that that's how

13

I perceived life and myself. As a result, this slanted perspective had infiltrated every single aspect of me, sending me down the path of overwork and exhaustion.

Determined to embrace the Divine Feminine more in my life, I left the regression and walked straight into the Glastonbury Goddess Temple, which happened to be right across the street. The Goddess Temple in Glastonbury is an emblem of one of the most popular reconstructions of goddess-based spirituality worldwide. Every year, it attracts hundreds of women and men, who attend its ceremonies and train to become priests and priestesses of the Goddess. That's what I was going in for as well.

Having previously attended their ceremonies and witnessed the depth through which they honoured the Divine Feminine, I thought that training to be a priest of the Goddess would be the perfect way to embrace the feminine aspect of Source. However, my conversation with one of the temple's priestesses soon made me realise that although I respected their Celtic traditions, they weren't part of my culture. It didn't feel authentic for a Greek merman to pretend to be a Celtic mage. Also, the hunch that got me into the White Spring Cave in the first place, the idea of finding the feminine from within the masculine, intrigued me. I knew I had to go deeper.

Thankfully, I didn't have to search much further. My desire to find balance was heard clearly by the Universe, and I'd taken physical action steps towards it. I showed up for me, and so the Universe had to show up for me, too. It did so that very night when, returning back to the little room I'd rented in Glastonbury, I wondered whether something similar to the Celtic goddess priestess training existed within my own Greek-Cypriot culture. I searched online, and to my surprise I found that the official council of the Greek pagans (the indigenous polytheistic religion in Greece, honouring the ancient gods and goddesses of the Hellenic pantheon) were running their first ever priesthood training course.

The Orthodox Christian church and the state had fought Greek pagans in both Greece and Cyprus for hundreds of years, and this was the first time in the modern history of Greek paganism that the Greek government had warmed to the idea of legalising their existence as a religion. The Priesthood Training Course was a big step towards breaking out of the patriarchal control that had smothered their voice for years, and marked their position in the world. The parallel between their history and mine was apparent, and I instantly knew it was the right direction for me.

## Divine Balance

In October 2017, I travelled to Athens, Greece, and became a priest of Hellenic Paganism. It wasn't what I expected it to be, but I say that in the best way possible. Although my personal goal following the past life regression was to embrace the feminine side of Source, the ancient Greek tradition was all about honouring the balance between the two. The very basis of ancient Greek religion, life and architecture was harmony, a perfect balance between the masculine and feminine aspects of things. Gods and goddesses were honoured in couples, and each god and goddess had both masculine and feminine aspects, maintaining this balance. Thus, by connecting to a feminine deity, you automatically honoured the masculine, too, and vice versa. Honouring just one side single-handedly was thought to upset that balance.

Although balancing masculine and feminine energy made logical sense, it wasn't easy for me to accept, which is something worth pondering. If you take a look at not just religion, but also politics, the economy and the whole of life, you'll notice that balance isn't as popular as polarity and division. These aspects of modern life work in cycles, swinging from one extreme to the other. There's hardly been a time in our world's recorded history when the economy, politics or religion functioned in a balanced way.

The basis of this polarity is our disconnect from nature, which is a pure extension of Source, and is therefore always, always in a state of balance. My Geography teacher used to tell me, 'It's not a matter of saving Planet Earth, but of saving the human race.' Mother Earth has outlived everyone who has inhabited her, and she'll keep on doing so regardless. There are processes to ensure that she maintains her balance, even if it means kicking us out. All the adverse modern atmospheric phenomena we are currently experiencing are a response to this. Humanity has created a polar, patriarchal culture that's out of balance with the laws of nature. We've tried to tell nature how life should be, rather than following her proven ways and wisdom, and as a result we're suffering.

Taking a look at religion and spirituality specifically, religion in Western civilisation has leaned towards the masculine side of Source. If we allow it to follow the same trajectory, it will eventually shift from masculine to feminine, reaching yet another state of imbalance, bringing forth new challenges and destruction. Accepting and honouring balance by trusting and following Mother Earth's ways, and therefore our soul's way, is the only way we can truly thrive.

The reason I was resistant to accepting this truth, despite consciously agreeing with it, has to do with the depth to which patriarchy is embedded in our world, which I touched on earlier. It's not easy for us to untangle the thousands of years of masculine-focused life that saturates our collective consciousness. What's easier than untangling that which isn't working is rebuilding what we know is working. In other words, the easiest way to end a negative cycle is to start building a positive one.

Rather than attempting to deconstruct the lifetimes of patriarchal spirituality that was embedded in me, I decided to take a leap of faith by turning my attention to, and investing my energy in, what I knew had always thrived by being in a state of balance: Mother Earth. Although my ego was resisting me giving my graduating oath at the end of the priesthood training, my soul screamed a loud and clear, 'Yes!' and, just like that, I stopped giving energy to a masculine past and started creating not a feminine future, but a balanced one.

Shortly after my trip to Athens and my commitment to a balanced life and spirituality, I expectantly received the calling to make a drastic change in my life that reflected these newfound beliefs. It was time for me to go back home; it was time to leave behind my masochistic work schedule and nature-deprived life in London and head back to Cyprus, where I would be able to work my light by focussing on my business full-time, and also nurture my light by connecting to Mother Earth, embracing feminine energy by living some more, and committing to the new phase on my spiritual path.

In essence, although I was returning to the place I was born, the home I was really going back to was Nature.

It wasn't until after I'd moved back to Cyprus that the word lightworker truly made sense to me. It became clear that working your light has to involve striking a balance between the masculine and feminine aspects of Source, as these relate to the practical aspects of life. The Divine Masculine and masculine energy are all about taking action and moving forward, whereas the Divine Feminine and feminine energy invite us to rest, listen to our intuition, surrender and allow things to come to us.

Neither is more important than the other, and both are essential for embodying our lightworker status and working our light in the truest sense of the word. In the following chapter, we'll delve into the specifics and present a brief history of lightworkers, and how you can truly and fully start working your light in your life.

## Chapter 2

# ASCENSION LIGHTWORKERS

*Lightworker: "Someone who wholeheartedly makes the decision to make the world a brighter place by being in it."*
*– Rebecca Campbell, Light is the New Black.*

Over their souls' journeys, lightworkers have incarnated as witches, healers, shamans, wise ones, mystics and spiritual seekers of all sorts. They have been burned at the stake, crucified for their beliefs, persecuted for practicing their magic and shamed for owning their light and speaking their truth. Yet, lifetime after lifetime, these brave souls have chosen to be reborn from the ashes, recuperate their strengths and come back time and time again, persisting and perfecting their skills and shining their light.

## Are You an Ascension Lightworker?

*Ascension Lightworkers* are a group of lightworkers who have chosen to incarnate on our planet over the past few decades. These are old, spiritually mature souls, who've come forth to assist in the ascension of our planet to a higher vibrational frequency; to help upgrade the earth's software, if you like.

Just as we individually have our personal journeys of ascension, so too do we collectively, and we're now on the cusp of transitioning to a new level of consciousness. This has been referred to as the New Golden Age, or the Age of Aquarius, but right now we're still in the midst of this transition, with an increasing number of people awakening to their spirituality and choosing to lead more loving, peaceful lives. The culmination of this new era will be energetically comparable to the Golden Age of Atlantis, in the sense that most of humanity will be aligned to their Source and awakened in their spiritual awareness and skills, working together to create heaven on earth.

Of course, light is only experienced when there's darkness to contrast it. The new era will also include darkness, in the sense of spiritually disconnected souls acting out in crime, corruption and violence, but there will be significantly less than what we experience currently.

## The Purpose of Ascension Lightworkers

Right now, you may be wondering, *How can we already be transitioning to this new vibrational era, when the darkness in our world seems to be getting stronger and more powerful than ever before?*

The purpose of ascension lightworkers has nothing to do with ensuring that light wins, for light has already won. Darkness has no source or beingness. It is but an illusory manifestation of a collective disconnect from light.

Over the course of modern history, the forces of light and darkness have intensified their presence on our planet with the aim of creating a big enough vibrational rift in consciousness. The aim of this is to create a strong enough desire to transition into the new paradigm.

Although destructive manifestations of darkness have increased in recent years, and crime, terrorism and environmental destruction seem to be the norm, so too have the positive manifestations of light. This is partly because it is the first time in human history that lightworkers have had the freedom to be themselves freely, fully and unapologetically. It's the first time in modern human history that there's little censoring of information, and the internet has made available a wealth of knowledge and opportunities that lightworkers can use to make a change.

This sentiment is best captured by Abraham-Hicks's quote, 'It's the best of times and the worst of times, because it's the most of times.' Adding to this statement, the purpose of ascension lightworkers is to help human consciousness ascend to the point where it's the best of times and the *bestest* of times, with just a few bad times. From there, it's just a matter of how high we choose to vibrate.

## A Brief History of Lightworkers

Older generations of lightworkers have known and felt their light, but often shied away from working it. The primary reason why they didn't do so was due to the patriarchal structures that have dominated human culture for the past six thousand years.

According to Gerda Lerner, American historian and leading expert in Women's History, in her book *The Creation of Patriarchy*, patriarchy started developing as early as the end of the Neolithic era and the beginning of civilisation, and involved the interplay of various socioeconomic and cultural factors.

The first patriarchal families were formed as the first humans acquired the notion of ownership. Men, therefore, wished to pass their herds down to their own blood progeny, insisting that women be virgins when married. Consequently, women's reproductive ability was increasingly seen as a village resource, turning women into a commodity. This notion was further enhanced when intertribal warfare expanded into large-scale wars, leading to women being captured and traded.

Gradually, throughout the years, the belief that women were lesser than men became more prominent, influencing all aspects of society, including religion and spirituality. This started with ancient Mother Goddesses being demoted in the pantheon of gods during the Neolithic era, and found its peak in the modern-day rise of Christianity and the Abrahamic religions, where the role of the Divine Feminine – the feminine aspects of Source – is demoted to being complementary, and even inferior to, the glory of a masculine God – the Divine Masculine, and masculine aspects of Source.

As a result of the rise of patriarchy and the dominance of masculine energy, lightworkers' purpose of maintaining the balance suffered significantly. Many lightworkers chose to suppress their purpose, dim their light and find comfort in the new masculine reality. Others dismissed masculine energy altogether and found comfort in feminine energy alone, nurturing their light in the closet and not working it.

Yet, a few courageous lightworkers did swim against the stream and worked their light brightly. These brave souls have laid the foundations for the rise of human consciousness we're working on right now.

Martin Luther King worked tirelessly to achieve greater equality for both men and women; Anne Frank, with her honesty and courage, filled the world with hope, affirming that, 'in spite of everything… people are truly good at heart;' Mahatma Gandhi dispelled the notion that feminine energy wasn't productive by employing non-violent demonstrations in his quest for Indian Independence; Helen Keller changed the perception people had about deafness and blindness, teaching that we all have something positive to contribute to the world. Alongside these brave lightworkers are many others whose stories went unwritten, but whose lightwork we experience in our freedom to be ourselves and shine our light freely today.

What's common among these trailblazing lightworkers is their commitment to taking real, physical, consistent action towards shining their light. They didn't just feel their desires, meditate on them and visualise the world being more equal and peaceful; they wrote books, spoke their truth, debated, campaigned and, as a result, shifted perceptions and changed the world. We don't just owe these lightworkers gratitude for their work, we owe them the continuation and fulfilment of what they started. It is our duty to heal our past wounds, nurture our light and rise up in the world with real, physical action, finishing what they started.

Although we're currently on the right path to doing so, it's easy to stray away from it. Our pursuit of dismantling patriarchy and restoring balance has led to the Divine Feminine rising once again. Lightworkers all over the world, whether they identify with the term or not, have helped to re-establish the importance of the Divine Feminine and feminine energy in general, in spirituality, society, economy and culture. There's still a long way to go before the Divine Feminine can claim its rightful seat next to the Divine Masculine, but a lot has already been achieved.

Yet, our thirst in raising the Divine Feminine – driven by thousands of years of having it be victimised, persecuted and suppressed by patriarchy – may result in yet another vibrational imbalance, this time favouring feminine energy. Many lightworkers have, consciously or not, chosen to victimise masculine energy altogether, and have dedicated their time and energy to nurturing their light without working it.

In their desire and passion to reinstate the importance of the Divine Feminine, they've completely disregarded the importance of masculine energy, and have discarded it from their daily functions altogether. As a result, many lightworkers falsely believe that nurturing light is the same as working it.

Sometimes, having something taken away from us for a long period of time creates such a strong desire to get it back that we lose sight of the end goal and the way to get there. In the case of masculine and feminine energy, we've lived in a patriarchal world for so long that we don't really know how a balanced world would look or feel. Having no reference point to lead our effort for change, we don't exactly know what steps we need to take to bring it forth.

So, we keep pushing for the rise of the Divine Feminine because we know that's what's missing, but, having lost sight of the big picture, we may be inadvertently creating a new energetic imbalance. Thankfully, we have access to that big picture each time we align to Source, because although our egos have forgotten it, our souls have never disconnected from it.

Whenever we journey within and find our connection to Source, we access this big picture. It may be hidden under layers of past hurts, traumas, programming and limiting beliefs, but it's always there and we can always *feel* it to some degree or another.

The collective purpose of ascension lightworkers is to find balance in the masculine and feminine energy within us, so that we can be present in, and act from, this balanced state and create change in society, religion, culture, the economy, politics and the world at large.

It's time to heal the traumas of past hurts, suppression, and persecution that patriarchy brought upon our soul, while at the same time reinstating our trust in the Divine Masculine and balancing the masculine and feminine energies within us. This way, we can join our brave lightworker ancestors in fulfilling their, and *our*, purpose as ascension lightworkers by ascending human consciousness.

Lightworker, you're no longer in danger of being burned, persecuted, shamed or ridiculed. The light has come, and it isn't going anywhere. You're free from the struggles of your past, and you have the freedom to express your light freely now.

Masculine energy isn't the bad guy anymore; it was never the bad guy in the first place. Abusing it has created some pretty messed up things in our world, but that's why you're here right now. This is your chance to make it right and use it in the way that it's meant to be used. This is your chance to balance the masculine and feminine energies within you, so you can experience your full lightworker potential and help make the world the loving, peaceful place you've dreamed of creating.

## The True Meaning of Lightwork

To help you understand more deeply what working your light means, let's deconstruct the term *lightwork*.

*Lightwork* is made up of two words:

*Light* embodies the Divine Feminine. It's your ability to receive inspiration from Source and enjoy the creative qualities of resting, retreating and nurturing yourself, while being idle and basking in the knowingness of the power of Source to create worlds.

*Work* embodies the Divine Masculine. It's your ability to form desires, take action, move forward, embark on new projects, create change, take risks and use your light in practical ways to bring desires into physical manifestation.

Patriarchy nurtured a culture of struggle, sacrifice and hard work, but that work has nothing to do with working the light, for work without light isn't light-work, but ego-work. When work isn't inspired by light, that is, it isn't 'inspired' action but rather 'forced' action, there's no substance to it.

When you combine light and work, you create magic; the action you take is inspired and it comes forth with purpose. As a result, it creates positive change easily and effortlessly (more on this in Chapter 21).

To get a more practical sense as to what working your light is and isn't, let's take a look at a few examples.

Working your light is **not**:

1. Meditating on world peace.

2. Sending healing energy to the world.

3. Shielding an area and people affected by a natural disaster.

4. Visualising the world being healed and peaceful.

5. Mentally sending love to a group of people.

Working your light **is**:

1. Writing books and articles that help people shift their mindset.

2. Creating courses and programmes that heal and transform lives.

3. Filming videos that teach, inform and inspire.

4. Writing letters to politicians.

5. Taking part in peaceful demonstrations.

6. Launching online and offline movements.

7. Not supporting unethical companies and products.

8. Speaking publicly about your vision and beliefs in a kinder world.

In essence, working your light has less to do with being idle and more to do with taking physical action towards the vision you hold in your heart and mind. Meditating, visualising and shielding are all powerful ways of nurturing light and feminine energy, and they're essential aspects of your path. However, these activities have little to do with working your light.

Simply put, the world isn't going to change by you knowing and affirming your light. The physical world we live in can only change through equally physical action steps.

Sometimes, lightworkers and spiritual seekers forget that we're not just love and light; we're love and light expressed in physical form. If we were just meant to be love and light, we wouldn't have come forth into this physical time-space reality. We chose to incarnate in a physical way so that we can do something with the love and light. We chose to come forth so that we can use the diverse, intricate, physical tools and processes that we've created in our world, to create physical change.

This is your wake-up call, lightworker. You're called to not just rise up, but to rise up and do something about it.

## Top-2 Blocks of Ascension Lightworkers

As a result of lifetimes of having to dim, hide or cease working your light altogether, yours and other ascension lightworkers' skills are quite rusty. Although you may be aware of our overarching purpose to create change, and truly want to work your light in real, physical ways, the traumas of past life hurts are very much still active within you, preventing you from finding, owning up to and fulfilling your personal life purpose.

Specifically, you're probably held back from following your purpose by one of the following two blocks:

1. **You don't know what your *specific* life purpose is.** Instead, you're merely familiar with our collective lightworker purpose of helping make a positive change in the world.

2. **You know your life purpose, but are held back by fear and limiting beliefs that keep you stuck.** As a result, you don't take consistent action towards your life purpose, or you tend to over-depend on the Universe for support.

In the pages that follow, you'll be introduced to tools and processes that will help you resolve these blocks, so you can fully own your purpose, regain your balance and take the action steps required to follow and fulfil it.

# Chapter 3

# YOUR FOUR PURPOSES

Everyone's life purpose draws from the soul's journey on planet earth. We come to the world with specific lessons that our soul wishes to learn in order to grow and advance spiritually. Many people are in the beginning of their soul's journey, so their life purpose revolves around personal fulfilment and mastering life on earth. Such life purposes could involve having a family, raising children and learning the meaning of love, friendship or forgiveness, or even something as simple as graduating high school.

What distinguishes lightworkers from other people is that we're already in a later stage on our soul's journey; we've already spent hundreds of lifetimes mastering being human and living life on earth. This doesn't make us perfect human beings by any means, nor does it mean that we don't have challenges in these domains during our current lifetime. It just means that we already have enough experience from our past lives to be able to deal with, and come out the other side of, tough life situations with more ease.

Instead, what lightworkers' souls really crave – what their purpose really involves – is not *mastering* life on earth, but *ascending and revolutionising* it. Lightworkers aren't here to maintain the status quo and learn to thrive within it;

they're here to change it and create new rules about how life on earth should be like.

As I mentioned at the end of the previous chapter, one of the biggest struggles lightworkers face is defining their life purpose in specific terms. What most lightworkers tend to think is that their life purpose is actually the lightworkers' collective purpose. Although knowing our collective purpose is helpful, it's not sufficient in fulfilling our specific life purpose.

In the first part of the book, we'll tackle this struggle head on. You'll find out that you actually have four different purposes, and you'll learn to distinguish between them and focus on defining your life purpose in a clear, one-to-two paragraph definition. Finally, I'll share with you my top tools for following your purpose, staying on track and eventually reaching fulfilment.

## Collective Purpose

Lightworkers' collective purpose has to do with ascending human consciousness and helping to make the world a more loving, kind and peaceful place. Ascending human consciousness means becoming increasingly connected to our authentic self, which is made up of both spirit and flesh. Ascending humans know that they're not just physical bodies, but that they're spiritual beings having a human experience. They understand that their ego and physicality aren't who they are, but are simply tools that their souls can use to teach a message of love.

Ascending humans don't reject or deny their physicality. They're at peace with it; they love it, actually. They honour and celebrate their humanity, but they know where it stands in the bigger picture of who they really are.

Lightworkers' collective purpose is to help bring forth this understanding to more people. It's our job to use the human skills we've nurtured over many lifetimes not to manipulate others into being kinder, more loving and peaceful, but to demonstrate to them what that means through our work and presence.

## Soul Realm Purpose

Soul realms are groups of lightworker souls that have a common purpose within the collective purpose; think of them as being similar to the different countries of the world. We're all humans, but we're divided into countries with unique customs, cultures, languages and beliefs. Although we all share in our humanity, we experience it in different ways according to our cultural influences.

Soul realms function in a similar way to countries. Lightworkers are divided into various groups of souls, with each group having unique characteristics, understandings, and purposes. In the same way that there are people of mixed race and a subsequent blending of cultural influences, so is there a mixing of soul realms and their qualities, too. In this sense, many souls can be a blend of two or more soul realms.

Soul realm purposes draw from the collective characteristics of each realm, and they involve creating large-scale change within a domain of earthly life. For example, realm purposes could be about preserving nature's wellbeing, advancing technology or developing alternative medicine. They can also be about helping humans at large develop the virtues required for ascension, such as developing sensitivity, forgiveness, self-love, tenacity, courage and kindness.

Although knowing your soul realm can give you an insight into what your life purpose is, it's not essential for homing in on your life purpose.

There are many categorisations of soul realms you can read about, but exploring them in full goes beyond the scope of this book. One way to get clarity on your soul realm is to read about the various realms and see which one(s) resonate most with you. Remember, you may be a blended realm, so don't be surprised if you relate to more than one.

Some of the most popular soul realms for you to explore are: Indigo Children, Rainbow Children, Starseeds, Incarnated Angels, Incarnated Elementals, Wise Ones and Shape Shifters.

Another way to get clarity on your soul realm, or blend of realms, is via past life regression. *Journey to Your Soul Realm* is a 90-minute online workshop, during which I guide you through exploring your soul realm past lives and determine your soul realm mix. You can access the workshop at GeorgeLizos.com/Shop

## Soul Purpose

Your soul purpose draws from your soul realm purpose, and it has to do with a purpose that your soul chose to fulfil over a series of lifetimes.

For example, if your soul realm's purpose has to do with environmental preservation, your soul's purpose could be about creating change within a specific field of environmentalism, such as maintaining the vitality of our oceans through marine conservation. The fulfilment of such a project could span hundreds of years, therefore your soul would need to incarnate several times until it successfully fulfils it.

Because they're so closely related, the soul purpose and life purpose are usually thought of interchangeably. However, it's worth understanding the difference between the two as a way of knowing where you are on your current soul journey and motivating yourself to fulfil your current life purpose, so that your soul can move on to the next phase.

Unlike the collective and soul realm purposes that take thousands of years to fulfil, your soul purpose only takes a few lifetimes, after which your soul ventures into yet another soul purpose adventure.

## Life Purpose

Your life purpose is a step towards fulfilling your soul purpose. It's a specific project, a smaller-scale change that'll get your soul closer to the finish line. It's so specific to your personality, talents, skills and abilities that without you, the world would be clueless as to how to go about fulfilling it. You're literally the only person who's qualified to do it.

Since your life purpose draws from your soul, soul realm and collective purposes, it still involves ascending human consciousness, but within a smaller niche field in society. For example, your life purpose could involve empowering women to make peace with food and their bodies, and through that help them to recognise the divinity within them and the food they eat; it could be about creating intuitive art that reflects people's dreams and desires, helping them see themselves through your art; or, your life purpose could be about teaching spiritual entrepreneurs essential financial skills that'll allow them to develop their businesses and amplify their message.

Each of these life purpose examples have larger-scale soul purposes and soul realm purposes attached to them, and they all lead towards helping a specific group of people ascend their consciousness. Thus, it all leads back to contributing to the fulfilment of our collective lightworker purpose of ascending life on earth.

Our power is always in the present moment, so we won't spend time specifying your collective, soul realm and soul purposes. Instead, all you need to be focussing on right now is your life purpose, as that is what you're here on this planet to fulfil. Your life purpose is the only venture you're able to undertake fully in this life, in order to fulfil your other three purposes.

In the following few chapters, we'll delve deeper into the characteristics of your life purpose, and I'll guide you through a practical 3-step process for specifying and defining it in a one-to-two paragraph definition. By the end of this part, you'll have a clear definition of your life purpose, as well as the tools that you'll need to start following it.

# Chapter 4

# HAPPINESS = PURPOSE

What if I told you that you're already following your life purpose to a certain degree, but are just not aware of it? And since you're not aware of it, you can't dedicate the necessary time required to fulfil it?

I had no idea that my life purpose involved becoming a spiritual teacher until I was 22 years old, yet I'd somehow started preparing myself for it long before then.

Spirituality has been my main passion since early childhood. As I mentioned previously, growing up I'd much rather spend my time hanging out with trees and flowers rather than with humans. This pretty much continued during my teenage years, which I spent delving into all sorts of magical subjects, from Feng Shui, Astral Projection, and Wicca to Meditation, Angel Communication and Divination. Spirituality was my favourite pastime, and I willingly passed on things like clubbing and hanging out with friends in favour of staying in and losing myself in New Age books, meditating with a new crystal or chatting to my angels and guides.

Spirituality has been a constant passion of mine throughout my life, yet I'd never even considered that it could be part of my life purpose. I was so brainwashed into believing that spirituality could only be a hobby and never a proper job, or that it was evil because it wasn't Christian, that it never crossed my mind that it could be the basis of what I was supposed to do.

## Happiness and Your Life Purpose

Things only shifted for me while walking home from university one day. It was my last year reading Geography at Bristol University, and I had an epiphany that changed everything after stumbling upon a nugget of wisdom that got me on the path to eventually finding and following my life purpose.

In that moment, I realised there was a direct correlation between happiness and our life purpose. That meant that whenever I was happy, I was following my life purpose, whether I was aware of it or not.

Here's how this works:

Let's start with the basis that God, Source, Spirit, the Universe, whatever you want to call it, is love. The emotion of love has a very high vibrational frequency, very similar to that of happiness. In other words, when you feel love, you're also happy and vice versa. Therefore, love and happiness feel pretty much the same.

Let's also agree that Source knows what our life purpose is, because it's Source! It's ever-present, all-encompassing and all-knowing.

Although we're physical extensions of Source ourselves, the degree to which we're consciously connected to it varies depending on our moment-to-moment human experience. The purest form of remembrance that we have of it is from when we were children, before we were indoctrinated into the ways of human life, and before our ego was fully developed. Take a look at newborn babies, for instance. Have you ever seen a judgemental or depressed baby? Not really, as we're born loving and happy, purely connected to the wisdom and knowingness of Source.

In understanding that Source is happiness and the keeper of our life purpose, and that our childhood was the closest we ever were to being fully connected to Source, we have a powerful formula for finding our life purpose. It's a simple formula that correlates human moments of happiness to our life purpose, urging us to shift our attention from our heads to our hearts and start seeking our life purpose through our emotions rather than our thoughts.

## Pleasure vs. Happiness

Before you start making connections between happy moments and your life purpose, it's worth taking some time to explore a common misconception people have regarding happiness.

What many people refer to as happiness is actually pleasure. Pleasure is an ephemeral emotion induced by an external factor. Eating, smoking, having a chat with a friend, taking a walk, exercising or having sex – all of these involve something external inspiring a positive feeling within you. Rather than happiness, this is pleasure.

Happiness isn't something you get through consuming or experiencing something, or by having an interaction with someone. Happiness is something you already *are*. Happiness isn't within you, it *is* you. Therefore, you can't find happiness anywhere outside of yourself, nor can you manufacture it with external substances and experiences. You can only remember happiness. When you remember happiness, you're naturally drawn to people, activities, circumstances and experiences that create pleasure, but also enhance the happiness that's already within you. These activities don't create happiness, they create pleasure, which enhances the happiness that already is you.

## Connecting the Dots

In this sense, identifying the moments in your life when you were naturally more aligned to your happiness, and exploring the activities, people, and experiences you were drawn to as a result, gives you specific and explicit clues as to what your life purpose is.

When you start understanding the correlation between happiness and your life purpose, you stop seeing your life as a series of random experiences that you ended up getting yourself into. Instead, you see your past as a perfectly orchestrated series of events designed to help you specify the activities and experiences that you're really meant to be focussing your time and energy on.

In the next chapter, I'll guide you through my proven 3-step formula for applying this understanding, digging into your past and connecting the happy dots that will lead you to your life purpose.

## Chapter 5

# 3 QUESTIONS TO YOUR LIFE PURPOSE

The following three questions explore your moments of happiness in three distinct time periods in your life. This will help you to acknowledge that, in truth, you've been following your purpose your entire life. In fact, you're following your life purpose right now; you just haven't allowed yourself to accept it yet.

To get maximum results out of this process, get out your journal and spend at least five minutes free-writing your answers to the questions. Don't overthink things, but instead go with the first thoughts that pop into your mind.

If you'd like me to personally guide you through the process, you can take my Life Purpose Intensive online workshop at GeorgeLizos.com/Shop

## *As a child, what did you want to be when you grew up?*

Think about the jobs or occupations that intrigued or excited you as a child. Why did you want to be that when you grew up? What specific aspects of this job excited you?

What was your experience or understanding of that job at the time? What did you wish you could accomplish as a result of being that person doing that job? Why did you choose this job over others? What was special about it?

Most importantly, how did the idea of doing this job make you *feel*? Sure, it was a pleasant emotion, but if you could choose more descriptive emotional words about it, what would these be?

As a child, you were unaware of the limits of the modern world and weren't yet indoctrinated into the rules and limiting beliefs that adulthood usually brings. As a result, your inner being was able to communicate with you clearly and emphatically. Your impulses, desires and preferences were all drawn from a deep knowing of your life purpose.

## What was the happiest time of your life?

Don't overthink this one, just close your eyes and think about your life as a whole. Which experience, event or time period was the happiest? Why was that? What were you involved in or doing that inspired so much positive emotion? What did you know about yourself, other people and the world that made you so happy? What did you accomplish? Who were you with? What hobbies or activities were you into at the time?

Spend some time taking a snapshot of your life at your happiest time, and then draw as much information as possible out of it.

If nothing comes to mind, divide your life into three time periods – childhood, teenage years and adulthood – and figure out which of the three was happiest. Then, home in on that period to identify pockets of happiness.

If more than one occurrence comes up, great! Write about them all. In all cases, try and extract as much detail as possible out of them, and link them to the emotions created as a result.

## What is the happiest time of your day?

Is it in the morning when you just wake up and have some quiet time to yourself? Is it while you're at work, getting stuff done and interacting with people? Maybe it's as soon as you come home to your pets, who are waiting for you with a large grin on their faces? Or, is it when your kids have gone to bed, and you finally get some alone time to curl up with a nice book or catch-up on your day with your partner?

Which is the happiest time within a usual day in your life? Most importantly, why is that so? Isolate the activities, thought patterns or routines you've set-up that make this time so precious to you.

In my experience with guiding people through this exercise, they usually get stuck on this question. Not because they can't remember what they do every day, but because they haven't been happy for a while. If this is you, that's OK. When you spend a long period of time feeling unhappy for any reason, it becomes the norm.

At the same time, when you don't generally experience a variety of contrasting emotions during your day for a long period of time, your ability to sense variance in emotion diminishes.

Maybe you haven't felt happiness for a while, but you have felt satisfaction, contentment or hope? If so, let these emotions guide the way. Your aim with this question is to find the most positive time period within your typical day. If hope is as positive as it gets, it's perfect! Go with it.

Having given each of these three questions at least five minutes of journaling time, in the next chapter you'll learn how to bring them together into your Life Purpose Declaration, a specific, two-paragraph definition of your life purpose.

# Chapter 6

# LIFE PURPOSE DECLARATION

Your Life Purpose Declaration is a specific, one-to-two paragraph definition of your life purpose. Rather than being a definite, concrete definition, it is rather a snapshot of what you're currently ready to know about your purpose. You'll amend and add more details to this definition as you take action towards it. I'll give you more guidance as to how to do so later on.

## Synthesise Your Answers

The first step towards coming up with your Life Purpose Declaration is to go through your answers for all three questions and identify common themes, words and emotions. Circle these and draw lines, making connections between your answers.

Is there a word that you keep going back to? Is there a subject or theme that keeps coming up? Are there certain activities, interests or hobbies that you keep talking about in all three answers? How about a state of being that you keep going back to?

Read between the lines as you go through this process, and don't necessarily interpret things literally. For example, wanting to be a nurse as a child needn't mean that your life purpose involves becoming a nurse. Conversely, what drew you to the nursing occupation might have been a need to nurture and to help people heal. Does this desire to help others show up in your answers for the other two questions, too? How so?

Reading between the lines is especially important when it comes to reading back to your answer to the first question, as although we're more attuned to our life purpose during childhood, our awareness of the world and our knowledge in general are limited. Therefore, the specific jobs that we wanted to do then won't truly represent our actual purpose, but the emotions and results that these jobs meant for us are almost always in alignment with our life purpose.

## Free-Write About Your Purpose

Once you've come up with a list of words, emotions, themes and topics that are common in all three of your answers, your journal will look like a spider web. This is gold. These connections hold clues to defining your life purpose in more specific terms.

Your next step would be to get into a meditative state and, using the connections you've made, free-write the definition of your life purpose. To make this effective, start with: *My life purpose is...* and then begin.

The key is to not overthink this. Rather than carefully thinking about and structuring your answer, just let your soul express all that it wants to say. Remember, your soul is already in alignment with your life purpose; it simply wants a platform to express itself. Let this process be it. Try to use as many of the words you've circled as possible, but don't worry too much about using them all.

Don't limit yourself as to how much you can write. Write as much and for as long as you want. By this point, and by answering the previous three questions, you'll have already brought yourself into a receptive state, through which your soul can communicate with you clearly. Enjoy this process.

## Craft Your Declaration

Finally, having given yourself the freedom to write freely about your life purpose, the final step in the process is to edit your answer into a one-to-two paragraph definition of your purpose.

Paying attention to the way you feel, go through your script and identify the parts and sentences that feel most in alignment with what your life purpose is. The operative phrase here is, 'the way you feel.' If it feels good, it is true.

Then, carefully craft the declaration of your life purpose while keeping the following in mind:

- Who or what are you here to serve?

- What will you help them achieve?

- How are you going to do it?

Crafting your Life Purpose Declaration is more of an art than a science, so keep changing and moulding your definition until you come up with something that feels good to you.

## Frame It, Share It, Revisit It

Once you have your declaration, put it somewhere you can see it daily. I have mine posted on the wall right in front of me while I work. Every single day, I read it out loud and remind myself why I'm here and what I'm here to do. Reminding yourself of your life purpose on a daily basis will keep you motivated to take action.

To further encourage yourself in following your purpose, you can even share it with a trustworthy, supportive group of friends or online community. A great place to do that is within my private Facebook group for empaths and lightworkers, *Your Spiritual Toolkit*. Sharing it with people who support you will keep you accountable for following it consistently.

It's also important to revisit this process and revise your declaration every six months. As you live and engage with the specifics of your life purpose, you'll get feedback as to whether or not you enjoy certain aspects of it. As you receive this emotional feedback, the specifics of your purpose will increase, decrease or change. Rather than stubbornly holding on to an outdated definition, be flexible enough to change it as you change (more on this in Chapter 8).

## Chapter 7

# HOW TO FOLLOW YOUR PURPOSE

Soon after you define your life purpose, you may find yourself too unmotivated or overwhelmed to take action. I get it, you have big dreams. You didn't come here to live a mediocre life, achieve mediocre things and make a mediocre impact. You're here to create big, positive change in the world. You're here to move energy and create something new.

It's a big task, and the immensity of it can hinder your creativity and motivation. Soon after you define your life purpose, your ego will come in and sabotage the heck out of you:

*Who do you think you are to even want to do that? You don't have enough training or experience. How can you help others when you haven't yet managed to help yourself? You're not strong enough to do this. You don't have enough money or energy to execute this. Who's going to trust you? You're a nobody. You're too ugly. You're not photogenic. You're not worthy. You're damaged. Stay here where it's comfortable. Play it safe.*

I don't need to be psychic to know what must be going on in your head right now. I know because I've heard all of it and more from my own ego, over and over again. The bigger our purpose, the harsher our ego's judgement will be.

## What is Ego?

Before we go any further let's spend some time understanding what the ego is, as it's only when you understand it that you can truly overcome its influence over you. There are two sides of you: your inner being and your ego. Your inner being is the spiritual aspect of you; the part of you that's constantly connected to Source, the entire Universe and every piece of consciousness within it. Your inner being knows it's powerful, limitless and all-knowing. Most importantly, your inner being knows what your life purpose is and how to fulfil it.

Your ego, on the other hand, is the physical, human side of you. It's not aware of your inner being and sees itself as disconnected from other people, the world, Source and the Universe. As a result of feeling disconnected, it fears for your wellbeing and strives to protect and keep you safe. Thus, your ego's sabotaging thoughts aren't malevolent in nature; they're simply part of its survival mechanism.

The ego isn't the bad guy, as many popular spiritual texts would have us believe. It simply has a different purpose. The aim, then, isn't to defeat or obliterate the ego, but instead to reassure it and reaffirm its sense of safety.

## One Daily Step

When you go from leading a small, safe life to declaring that you're ready to create big change in the world and in your life, the ego panics. There's too much risk involved; it cannot handle it. So, it does whatever it takes to keep you where you are. That's where the limiting thoughts come in.

What if, instead of declaring to the ego that you're about to create massive change, you simply declare that you wish to take smaller steps towards change? Do you think your ego will be equally terrified of change then?

Long ago, I discovered that taking smaller steps towards my purpose was enough to reassure my ego of its safety, while still getting me closer to fulfilment. Therefore, instead of taking massive action, like quitting my job and focussing on my purpose full-time, which would absolutely terrify my ego, I committed to taking a single, small step towards it every day.

One daily action step towards your purpose is enough to create waves. What's important is that you're consistent with it. Your small, daily steps will gather momentum, and as you show up for you, the Universe will show up for you, too. The energy that you put into these steps will eventually come back to you in people, experiences and opportunities, all lining up for you to take the next step and then the next one, and yet another one after that, until you're eventually following your purpose more fully.

The more steps you take, the more you train your ego to accept change. Eventually, as your ego begins to feel safer, the negative self-talk will decrease and you'll be able to take bigger steps, even multiple daily ones, and your purpose will unfold naturally.

Just don't try and do it all at once. Don't shock your ego. You're here for the journey, not the destination. Enjoy it.

# Chapter 8

# YOUR PURPOSE WILL CHANGE AS YOU CHANGE

'When I grow up, I want to be a singer.'

If you asked my parents, or anyone who knew me as a child, teenager or young adult, they'd tell you that my purpose would involve singing or performing in some way. I won my first singing competition at 10 and starred in musicals all throughout my school years. I even got a diploma in classical singing.

Later on, at university, I decided that it was time for me to get serious about my purpose in performing arts. For an entire year, I prepared to audition for a Masters in Musical Theatre, working with a professional actor to get my monologues ready, taking tap, ballet and contemporary dance classes to rock the dance workshop I'd have to attend, and polishing the audition songs that I'd worked on for years (*Glee's* Rachel Berry was my muse).

Then, one day, while heading home from a lecture, it hit me: *Why on Earth would I be a Musical Theatre actor? I'm meant to be a spiritual teacher.* It was an instant, unexpected mental shift that led me down a completely different path than I'd initially intended. In an instant, what I'd spent my entire lifetime up to that point thinking was my life purpose suddenly seemed insignificant.

Although I was dumbfounded by this unexpected change in my beliefs and desires, the emotional certainty I felt about it was unequivocal, and I had to trust it. That's when I realised an important lesson in following our life purpose...

## The Masks We Wear

Our purpose will change as we change. From a young age, the world teaches us to be consistent in our commitments and desires. We're taught to mould masks for ourselves and wear them with pride; we're put into boxes and are expected to stay in them forever; we get labelled the Creative Type, the Music Kid, the Science Geek, the Maths Freak, etc. This helps people to 'get' us, and gives us a sense of belonging and acceptance.

There's nothing wrong with having these labels, as it is our human nature to compartmentalise ourselves and the world around us. What's problematic is letting these labels go beyond describing us to rigidly defining us. When we get so hooked on other people's approval and expectations of us, we deprive ourselves of the ability to change and grow. Instead, we spend years wearing a persona that feels safe and is accepted by others, preventing us from embracing new aspects of ourselves.

## You Change, Constantly

You are different with every year, month, week, day, hour, minute and second that passes. Think about it; you're a thinking and feeling human being. Every thought you have, and every emotion you feel, changes you in some way. In time, the thoughts add up to beliefs and your emotions add up to action steps, all changing who you are.

If you're constantly changing, why would your purpose remain the same?

I can hear you thinking, *George, I thought that my life purpose was a specific action step towards fulfilling my soul purpose. How could it change?*

What we perceive as our life purpose shifting and changing is really our life purpose constantly revealing more of itself to us, based on how much of it we're willing and able to perceive and accept at any point. In truth, our life purpose is fixed and clearly defined; the degree to which we can perceive it isn't.

Let's take my case as an example. For years, I wanted to be a performing artist, not out of a selfish need to gain fame and recognition, but because what excited me the most about performing was getting to see people smile. I revelled in seeing the transformation of an audience from sad and grumpy to happy and uplifted by the end of a show.

Therefore, what I truly cared about with performing was helping people heal, which is not very different from the spiritual work that I do now. The essence of my purpose had always been the same; what *was* different was its expression and my ability to perceive it. A more accurate way to communicate this chapter's lesson, then, is that the *expression* of your life purpose will change as you change.

## Chapter 9

# YOU CANNOT FAIL ON YOUR LIFE PURPOSE

Let me tell you about the most unfortunate (and quite funny) day of my life.

I was in my second year of university and, fuelled by the fact that I was away from home in a different country and coming on my own, I allowed myself to indulge in the common student partying culture. To me, that involved a weekly routine of getting drunk and going clubbing on Saturday nights.

Week after week, I'd abuse alcohol on Saturday evening and then wake up the following day feeling guilty about it, before promising myself that I'd never do it again. However, I never kept my promises until I was left with no other choice but to do so.

You see, Spirit was sending me signs all along – signs that I was consciously receiving and mindlessly ignoring. The message was clear: 'Quit drinking and dedicate yourself to your spiritual practice!' I wish I'd followed these signs earlier.

One evening, while getting ready for my usual drunken night of partying, I accidentally stepped on a burning-hot hair-straightening iron that my friend had left on the floor, burning my foot. Long story short, it had me in bed for a week with a huge blister on my foot. I later popped the blister prematurely, causing an infection that had me limping for a month.

Needless to say, that was the last time I got drunk on a Saturday night. In fact, it was years before I took another sip of alcohol!

## The Signs Will Get Bigger

The reason I'm going to such great lengths to share the gruelling details of this story is to communicate a lesson I wish I'd learned earlier, and that you'd certainly benefit from learning sooner rather than later, too.

There are two conditions that will guarantee you'll fulfil your life purpose:

1.   Accepting your lightworker status.
2.   Finding and defining your life purpose.

At all times, you have around you angels, spirit guides, elementals and other spirits, all trying to grab your attention and point you towards finding and following your life purpose.

Source's single purpose is to help us fulfil ours, because we're at the forefront of expanding consciousness. Whereas

Source is immaterial, and thus limited in its creative potential, our physicality and ability to focus gives us the advantage of creating deliberately.

Being lightworkers, our ability to deliberately create is heightened, as we're aware of the laws of the Universe and have come here to create big, positive change in the world. You can imagine the excitement this brings to Source.

When your spirit guides realise that you know you're a lightworker who has done the work needed to define your purpose, they won't let you fail. They'll harass you with signs until you pay attention and take action towards following your purpose. The signs will get bigger and bigger and bigger until you're in bed, unable to move, with a huge blister on your foot that forces you to think about your purpose. That's when you'll finally make the commitment to follow it fully.

## You Are Guided

There's tremendous relief in realising that Source has your back. As you come to this realisation, allow the overwhelming fear around following your life purpose to dissipate.

There's nothing to be fearful about. No matter the scale of your purpose, you have with you at all times a group of all-powerful spiritual beings, orchestrating the perfect set of circumstances to ensure that you get there. You have friends in higher places co-creating with you, so to speak.

The only job you have is to look out for the signs and then have the courage to follow them. You'll learn how to receive clear signs from your guides in Chapters 30 and 31.

# Chapter 10

# IT'S NOT YOUR PURPOSE

I'm a control freak. I've struggled with this my entire life. From a young age, I'd try to control my thoughts, emotions and behaviour in an attempt to fit in and find the acceptance I so longed for. Although I've healed this control tendency to a large degree over time, it kicks in when I get stressed out, overwhelmed or out-of-tune with my inner being.

As a result, I start controlling and micromanaging every aspect of my life and purpose. I get upset when others feel dissatisfied with me and desperately try to win them back. I push through my feelings of being overwhelmed and work the extra hours until I've ticked off every single task on my to-do list. I'm the kind of person that has weekly, monthly and quarterly goals. In fact, I plan my entire year in advance.

Now, there's nothing wrong with being organised, and my systems ensure that I work my light efficiently. Things only go awry when I start depending too much on myself for getting things done, and don't allow myself to be held and helped by the Universe, too.

Time and time again, I've ignored my body's messages and allowed my controlling tendencies to get out of hand.

Every single time, I find myself on my knees, hands stretched out at my altar, tears running down my cheeks, asking Source to envelop me in its warm embrace, take the struggle away and assume control of the situation.

Source always shows up for me, and I feel held, protected and guided almost instantly. Then, invariably, I sit there wondering, *Why didn't I let go sooner?*

## It's Not Your Purpose

In time, I've come to realise that the easiest way to surrender control is by accepting that our purpose isn't really ours.

Think about it; you're a physical extension of Source, incarnating into a physical body with a specific mission to accomplish. Although, from your limited ego perspective, you may perceive yourself as a disconnected human being, with no connection to other people or the Universe itself, from your inner being's perspective, you know that you're one with Source.

In the knowingness of your interconnectedness, you realise that your purpose doesn't belong to you; it belongs to the wholeness of what Source is. You are simply the physical conduit through which this purpose can be fulfilled.

If it's not your purpose, but God's purpose, that means fulfilling it isn't entirely under your control. It's *God's* job to provide the guidance and action steps required to bring your purpose into life; *your* job is to do your best to be in alignment with your inner being, so that you can receive the guidance and be a co-operative component of the manifestation process.

## The Most Powerful Surrendering Process

When you catch yourself trying to control people and situations, replacing alignment with action and trying to play God, take a step back and get on your knees.

I mean this literally. The act of getting on your knees to pray is the most powerful form of surrender. Your body is your ego's most emblematic tool, and when you submit it to the ground, you symbolically tell your ego that it's powerless in the face of Source. You declare to your ego that it's got no place trying to play God, thereby opening yourself up to the guidance of your inner being.

In that moment of pure surrender, a power higher than yourself must flow in to carry the struggle away and replace it with peace. Eventually, once you've allowed yourself to shed the struggle and reach a state of ease, the divine guidance you've been asking for must flow through.

Your spirit guides will show up in whichever way makes most sense to you, imparting guiding thoughts and impulses that will signpost you towards the action steps that you need to take in order to perform more fully in following God's purpose.

# Chapter 11

# Your Unicorn Spirit Guide

I first became captivated by unicorns when they showed up in a Map History class that I was taking at university. As I opened the *mappamundi* I was studying, I was instantly mesmerised by the exquisite iconography of the Middle Ages, feeling compelled to anxiously peruse the elaborate symbolism, peculiar plants and wild animals depicted. Then, as I was eagerly trying to drink it all in, I glimpsed the horned creature in the top-right corner.

The professor's voice gradually faded into a distant whisper, and all I could hear, all I could see and all I could think of was the elusive being staring at me from the lightly creased paper. Under it, the calligraphic inscription read: *Unicorn*.

From that day onwards, I developed an inexplicable obsession with unicorns. I'd read books about quests to find and capture these elusive creatures, studied the various iconographic representations in which they were featured and immersed myself in the New Age concepts of them.

My unicorn journey led me to teaching *Unicorn Bootcamp*, an online course focussed on connecting with unicorns in order to get clear on our life purpose, as well as teaching about unicorns in the *Elemental Healing™ Practitioner Course* that I co-created with my friend and author of *Unicorn Rising*, Calista.

Working with unicorns, and specifically with my Unicorn Spirit Guide, was key to both finding and following my purpose. In this and the following chapters, I'll teach you how to establish your own relationship with your Unicorn Guide, with the aim of receiving actionable guidance on following your life purpose.

## A Brief History of Unicorns

To fully understand the symbolism, essence and presence of unicorns, let's briefly explore the history of unicorns through time.

Intriguingly, the first mention of unicorns came not in myth, but from the Greek physician and historian, Ctesias of Cnidus, writing in the 4th century BC, describing them as resembling an Indian ass with a white body, red head, blue eyes and a 28-inch long horn.

Later, a mistranslation of an animal referred to as a *reem* in the Hebrew version of the Old Testament to *monokeros* (unicorn) in the Greek version corroborated Ctesias' unicorn, launching an obsessive quest to find an animal so important that it was mentioned in the Bible. As a result, in the years that followed, unicorn poems were written, stories were created and artwork was commissioned.

The unicorns were glorified and associated with qualities such as strength and power, but also grace and poise. Capturing a unicorn was supposed to bring luck, prosperity and happiness, while the unicorn horn, the alicorn, was said to cure all illnesses. In fact, fake alicorns (which were really the tusks of narwhals) were sold for astronomical prices in the Middle Ages.

While these early writings launched the unicorn myth and the obsessive quest to find and capture it, natural historians and scientists eventually concluded that these unicorn accounts didn't describe a single animal, but rather a chimera of three different animals: the kiang, the chiru and the wild yak.

What's fascinating is that even after the unicorn myth was discredited, the belief in unicorns' existence and the desire to experience their magic persisted through time. One New Age theory suggests that unicorns *did* walk our planet as flesh and bone, but had to ascend to a higher dimension due to the toxic energy here, while another presents them as ascended horses.

The popularity of and interest in unicorns is so timeless and prevalent over the course of human history, trying to figure out whether they are real or not becomes irrelevant. What begs the question instead is, why has the unicorn carried such significance in so many cultures around the world for so long?

## The Spiritual Significance of Unicorns

Exploring unicorn history and symbolism over the years, it's not hard to identify a common thread in the various ways that they have been portrayed. Depicted as strong and powerful, but also gentle and graceful, the unicorn epitomises a balanced being that stands tall in its authenticity. The health, happiness, success and prosperity that capturing the unicorn would bring were all outcomes of these inner states of balance and authenticity.

For thousands of years, we obsessed over capturing a magical creature that would cure our illnesses, fix our finances and solve our problems, not realising that the creature we'd been searching for was always within us. The unicorn has always been real and will always be real as a symbolic and spiritual extension of our soul, balanced in masculine and feminine energy and unapologetically authentic. Our soul has turned itself into a horned horse in an effort to grab our attention, and through stories, tapestries, songs and statues, inspired a quest to capture it.

Although we've taken on the quest and searched for it tirelessly throughout the years, we've skipped looking in the single place where it's always resided, within us.

## Your Unicorn Spirit Guide

In this sense, your Unicorn Spirit Guide is a spiritual extension of your soul, perfectly balanced in masculine and feminine energy and unapologetically authentic.

Your Unicorn Guide is constantly with you, gently prodding you to embrace the Divine Feminine qualities of self-care, nurturing, trusting your intuition and taking a break; very much needed in a society that constantly pushes us to be more and do more. Your Unicorn Guide also reminds you that Divine Masculine energy isn't about abusing work and taking action, but rather that this creative energy should be used in a balanced way to support the Divine Feminine and create positive changes in your life and in the world.

Your Unicorn Guide embodies your authentic self and your life purpose. It knows your unique strengths, talents, abilities and personality characteristics, and guides you to use them in finding and following your purpose. It's been sending you signs through your favourite unicorn quotes, the unicorn merchandise you buy and the unicorn imagery you share on social media. Now that it's got your attention, it's here to guide you on your journey towards becoming fully yourself.

## Chapter 12

# UNICORN MEDITATION: FLY TO YOUR PURPOSE

Of all the spirit guides that guide you on your journey, your Unicorn Spirit Guide is the best equipped and most passionate about helping you find and follow your life purpose. Remember, your unicorn is a spiritual extension of your soul, which means it is one with your soul and therefore in alignment with your life purpose and the way to fulfil it.

I still remember the first time I met my unicorn, Xeros. Looking into his eyes was like seeing the highest vibrational version of myself. His presence alone raised my vibration and provided me with a sense of trust, ease and safety. Right then and there, I knew I was being guided, and in our subsequent sessions together, he led me to the perfect roadmap for following my purpose fearlessly.

The following meditation will help you to meet your unicorn, and then go on a progression journey to see yourself fulfilling your life purpose in this lifetime. By projecting to a future point in time when you're already following your purpose, you'll be able to see how that looks, so that you can guide yourself there. At the end of this meditation, you'll use your experience to amend or add to your Life Purpose Declaration.

Here are the steps to the meditation:

1. Close your eyes, breathe deeply, relax your body and come into a meditative state.

2. With your mind's eye, visualise a tiny dot of golden light in the centre of your heart. Your heart is the doorway to your soul, and the golden light lets it in.

3. With every inhale, visualise the golden light growing outwards until it fills up your chest and body, and then extends outwards to envelop your aura. Bask in the energy of your soul for a few minutes.

4. Mentally call upon your Unicorn Guide to make its presence felt. Once you've saturated your body and aura with the energy of your soul, your unicorn must show up.

5. You may see, hear or feel your unicorn joining you. Spend some time getting used to its high-vibe energy. Ask for a name and get to know him/her in the same way you do when you make a new friend.

6. Your unicorn invites you to take a journey together. Jumping on its back, you fly over a beautiful rainbow. When you reach the other end of the rainbow, you'll find yourself at a point in time where you're already fulfilling your life purpose.

7. Spend as much time as you need to explore what this looks like and take it all in. What are you

involved in during this future point in time? What do you do for a living? What change are you making in the world? Through what medium are you doing so? How does it feel? Register all the details.

8. When you're done exploring, jump back on your unicorn and fly back over the rainbow to the present time.

9. Thank your unicorn for guiding you through this journey, and know that you can come back to it whenever you need.

10. Gradually, come out of meditation.

You can download an expanded audio recording of this meditation at GeorgeLizos.com/LGW

As soon as you're done with the meditation, take out your Life Purpose Declaration and amend or add to it any details or information that came up during your meditation.

# PART II

# NURTURE YOUR LIGHT

# Chapter 13

# MADE OUT OF LOVE AND LIGHT

We're made out of love and light.

I'm sure you've seen this phrase thrown around casually by spiritual teachers, in your conversations with friends, Instagram memes and in spiritual communities both online and offline. We take this for granted as the true essence of who we are, but to what degree do we truly understand these words?

Let's ponder on the concept of love and light for a while, and try to gain a deeper sense of what it really means.

## Made Out of Love

When most of us say this, we mean that the essence of that which we are - our soul, inner being and authentic self - is a loving one, but how can we be so sure of that?

The closest proof we can get as to what emotion our true essence has are newborn babies. If we assume that we come from Source, then in the moment we are born, we're the closest we can get to our creator.

With this in mind, have you ever seen a depressed baby? How about an angry or resentful one?

Don't think too hard, because the answer to both questions is no. Sure, babies experience negative emotions when their needs aren't being met, but are any of these negative emotions chronic ones?

Newborn babies, having just come forth from Source and not yet being indoctrinated into our limiting thoughts and beliefs, emanate this pure-positive energy – an emotion that can best be described as the emotion of love.

From this perspective, it's safe to assume that if babies who have just come forth from Source emanate the emotion of love, this must be the vibrational frequency that Source has. By that logic, this is what being one with Source, and therefore ourselves, feels like.

## Made Out of Light

Being made out of love is easy to accept, since it's an emotion we can feel in our body and translate into words, but what about light? How did we come up with that one? How can our physical bodies be made out of light?

According to quantum physics, when you zoom in on every single piece of consciousness in the world, the smallest particles you'll find – the atoms – behave like waves or vibrations. These carry energy, which we perceive as light. In other words, you could say that our physical bodies are quite literally lit up!

Although accepting that we're made out of love is more of a safe assumption, the fact that we're made out of light is pure science. More astonishingly, since every single piece of consciousness is made out of light, it means that we're all interconnected within a giant web of energy. We're all one, so to speak.

## Made Out of Love and Light

Putting the two together, we're non-physical love and light expressed in physical form. When we allow the all-knowing power of love, and the light that connects us to all life, to flow freely through us, we're lit up. These two forces work together to inspire us with guidance, orchestrate experiences and co-create circumstances that allow us to follow and fulfil our life purpose in order to live happy, abundant lives.

The best thing about knowing our true essence is realising that no matter how disconnected we may be from Source, we can never completely lose our connection to it. No matter the negative emotions you may be feeling or the limiting thoughts and beliefs you have, and no matter how much you've kept yourself from experiencing your true essence, your connection to it can never be severed.

You are love and light, always. You can stray from home, but your connection to it will always lead you back. Isn't this such a relief? Isn't it a relief to know that no matter what you're going through and no matter what may happen, you'll always return back to love and light?

## Nurturing Love and Light

Although your connection to love and light can never be lost, the ability to increase the flow of love and light flowing through you at any point is entirely in your own hands. Nurturing love and light by deliberately taking the time to increase the flow of it takes practice, focus and commitment.

The degree to which you nurture your love and light is very similar to working out. When you exercise consistently for a month, you see noticeable changes in your body. If, on the other hand, you exercise inconsistently, you'll hardly notice a difference. At any moment in time, your physical body has the potential of being either toned and strong or loose and weak.

Your love and light are the same way. Whenever you take the time to nurture them, they'll grow, and so will your connection to Source and your capacity to receive guidance that'll allow you to move forward towards your life purpose.

In the following chapters of Part Two of this book, we'll focus on practices you can use to consciously and consistently nurture your love and light, so that you can receive the divine guidance to work it and create positive change in the world. For simplicity purposes, I'll refer to 'nurturing love and light' as 'nurturing your light,' but the meaning is the same.

## Chapter 14

# YOUR SPIRITUAL PRACTICE

Your spiritual practice doesn't have to be spiritual. This is a big misconception that keeps many lightworkers from having a daily practice. Overwhelmed with the plethora of spiritual modalities, lifestyles and processes, we feel like we have to act and dress up in a certain way to be spiritual.

To someone just starting out on their spiritual path, the image of a spiritual practice may look like long hours of silent meditation, lighting up incense, praying to statues of goddesses and chanting mantras that don't really make much sense to them. Although these methods may well be part of your spiritual practice, they needn't be.

To truly understand the meaning of having a spiritual practice, let's ponder on what spirituality is. If, as we discussed in the previous chapter, we're made out of love, the aim of the spiritual path would be to nurture that love. From this perspective, spirituality can be defined as the practice of choosing love every step of the way.

Your spiritual practice, then, is simply the practice of love. Not just the emotion of love, but the vibration of love in general. Happiness is also at the vibrational frequency of love, and so are many other emotions such as enthusiasm, fun, playfulness, elation and more.

*(In this chapter, and on many occasions in the book, I'll focus on the emotion of happiness instead of love, as it matches very closely the vibration of love without the connotations of attachment and expectation that the emotion of love usually comes with. This is also done to separate the different expressions of love, such as romantic, friendship, familial and self-love from the pure vibration of spiritual love.)*

The activities that you choose to include in your spiritual practice don't need to be spiritual, in the sense that you don't need to use any complicated spiritual modalities, mantras, mudras, candles, incense or yoga mats. You simply need to choose activities that make you happy and commit to them.

## Three Components to Your Spiritual Practice

Specifically, here are the three components that your spiritual practice needs to have in order to be effective in nurturing your love and light:

1. **Happiness:** Your spiritual practice has to be a happiness practice. What lights you up? It could be meditation and yoga, but it could also be walking your dog, dancing, singing, writing down things that you're grateful for or listening to an inspirational talk or some music – literally anything.

2. **Consistency:** Your spiritual practice has to be a daily practice, and it has to be at a specific time each day. If it's not, then it's less a practice than a hobby. Committing to your practice this way is

important, because it shows your seriousness in nurturing your light and following your life purpose. When you show the Universe that you're serious about showing up for you, it gets serious about showing up for you in return.

3. **Duration:** Your spiritual practice should ideally last between 15 to 30 minutes, if not longer. Remember the workout analogy? If you exercise for 5 minutes daily, you'll get some benefit, but no visual transformation. If, on the other hand, you increase your time of exercise to at least 15 minutes, you'll be sure to expect noticeable changes to your physique. Your happiness and light work the same way. The more you nurture them, the better results you'll see in your outlook, energy and ability to receive inspired action guidance.

## Crafting Your Spiritual Practice

When you first start on your lightworker journey, it's better to keep things simple. Choose three activities that inspire within you the emotion of happiness and commit to them daily, for at least 15 to 30 minutes. The best time to do your spiritual practice is first thing in the morning, as the way you start your day sets the tone for the rest of it. However, you're free to do it at any other time that makes sense for you, too.

Just like with all changes, your ego will at first resist this. Remember, the ego wants to protect you, and any change threatens its control over you. It'll come up with a thousand excuses to prevent you from starting your spiritual practice.

Here are some common ones:

*I don't have time to do it.*

*I have to take the kids to school.*

*I'm too tired in the morning.*

*I'm too sleepy to do it in the evening.*

*I can't concentrate enough to meditate.*

*I'm already feeling happy today, so I'll skip my practice.*

*I'll do it later.*

Here's some tough love for you, lightworker. If you have time to feel like crap, you have time to feel good, too. Every day, you're faced with two choices: feel good or feel bad. Having a spiritual practice is guaranteed to make you feel good, whereas not having one leaves it up to chance. So, will you take your chances, or will you consciously and deliberately choose happiness every single day? Your choice.

## Your Emergency Practice

Let's face it, we're humans, not machines. Despite our commitment to having a spiritual practice, there will come days where we're not really feeling up to doing it, or we are not in a position to do it fully, e.g. when we're on holidays, travelling or staying with other people.

In these cases, I like to have an emergency, or non-negotiable, spiritual practice. This is a toned-down version of my full practice, which is just enough to maintain my current level of love and light and not let it get depleted.

To me, this means stripping down an elaborate three-hour spiritual practice to a 15-minute meditation. That's all it takes to help me establish my connection to Source at the beginning of the day and get me started on the right foot.

What would this be for you? What is a shorter practice that you're willing to commit to doing no matter the circumstances of your life? Even if it's a 5-minute meditation, dancing to a song or writing down ten things that you're grateful for, it's still enough to awaken and sustain your light.

## How to Deal with Relapse

At some point in your spiritual journey, you're going to relapse. Let's take this for granted. You'll be hungover after a night out drinking and won't do your spiritual practice for a week, you'll have that early morning meeting that throws you off schedule or you may need to run family errands and so simply need all the time you can get. That's OK. The spiritual journey is not a journey of perfection, but one of progress.

If, like me, you tend to be hard on yourself when things get out of hand, you may find yourself being overly self-judgemental and self-pitying. Your ego will love to rush in and say, 'I told you so,' encouraging you to let this *spiritual thing* go and return to playing it safe.

An alternative way to handle relapse is by following these steps:

1. **Accept that you've relapsed.** Don't try to deny it and over-spiritualise it with fluffy affirmations and excuses. Be real with yourself. You've relapsed. Own it, and then focus on a resolution.

2. **Forgive yourself.** Realise that relapsing is part of being human, and you're 100% allowed to do so. It doesn't make you less spiritual or less worthy. The aim is not to be lit up 24/7, but to know how to get yourself there at will.

3. **Start slow.** Don't overwhelm yourself with a one-hour spiritual practice the following morning. Allow yourself to ease back into your practice with a single activity, and then eventually add more activities to it. If you rush it, you may shock your ego with too much of a change, which will flare up its sabotage instinct.

The most important thing to remember when crafting your spiritual practice is that it has to be fun enough to inspire within you the emotion of happiness. If at any point your practice feels like a chore, go back to the drawing board and make adjustments until it feels just right.

## Chapter 15

# MEDITATION HACKS

If I had to strip down this book to a single practice that'd allow you to nurture your light, it'd be meditation. Meditation is the simple act of quieting your mind from thought and reaching for a state of peace.

Chatting to lightworkers about meditation down the years, it seems as though their biggest block to adding meditation to their daily practice has been their inability to quiet their minds from thought completely. That's because it's not really possible to do so.

I've been meditating daily for over 10 years, and it's rare that I'm able to be completely thoughtless for more than a few minutes at a time. You see, our minds were made to think, so trying to enforce thoughtlessness goes against their very nature. That's why, rather than trying to obliterate thought, meditation is about lessening it.

## How Meditation Works

To understand the benefit of this, let's ponder the mechanics of meditation and the way in which it works to help nurture our light.

Thoughts create emotions, therefore any emotion we feel is backed up by a thought or group of thoughts – a belief. As you've learned in previous chapters, nurturing light is all about reaching for the emotion of love, an emotion that we were born with and that defines our very essence.

If we're made out of love, we needn't try too hard to remember it. All that's required is to remove the obstacles that prevent the natural flow of love within us. These obstacles are none other than the limiting thoughts and beliefs that we've nurtured over many years. Meditation, then, allows us to think less of those limiting thoughts and beliefs, thus allowing the love that *is* us to flow through our mind and body unhindered.

As we release thought and allow the love within us to be realised, we soften the boundary between our physicality and spirituality and allow the blending of our two natures. As a result, we achieve the perfect balance between our two sides, which allows for an effortless communication of the knowing of our life purpose and the guidance towards following it.

## How to Meditate

There are many ways to meditate. Googling the word will yield hundreds of meditation techniques, developed by various cultures over thousands of years. Although I love the bells and whistles of the various meditation practices, I believe that simplicity yields the most powerful results.

As I mentioned earlier, since our minds are made to think, it'd be pointless to try to completely obliterate our thoughts. What's more effective is thinking less or giving our minds something small and insignificant to think about; something that doesn't create negative emotions and allows our vibration to naturally rise to our authentic state.

My suggested way to meditate, for the purpose of this book, would be to sit in a comfortable position every morning for 15 minutes, and to give your mind something small to think about. Meditating in the morning is ideal, as you wouldn't have been introduced to significant negative emotions or experiences by that point, making reaching for alignment easier. Meditating in the morning also sets the tone for the rest of the day.

Since this meditation process involves a degree of thinking, I've included four ways, or hacks, that can help you achieve this. These are easy to practice and will help you ease into this meditation practice. Give them a try and see how they resonate with you. Take the ones that you enjoy and adjust them to fit in with your lifestyle and personal preferences.

## 1. Use Simple Mantras or Affirmations

An easy way to think less is by mentally repeating a mantra while you breathe, such as *Om* or *Sat Nam* (or make up your own). I like to use my favourite affirmation, 'All is well,' or simply a word like 'silence,' which I coordinate with my inbreaths and outbreaths. It gives my mind something to think about, letting it feel useful in performing its natural function, while at the same time allowing my vibration to rise because I'm not blocking it with the limiting thoughts and beliefs that often occupy my mind.

## 2. Listen to Sounds in Your Environment

Another way to give your mind something small to think about is by concentrating on the various sounds of the environment you're in. This could be the ticking of the clock, the sound of the air conditioning, the birds chirping happily in the garden or even a tractor in the construction site nearby. Ideally, find something that's constant and consistent to focus on, and which won't pique your interest or distract you in any way.

## 3. Focus on a Physical Object

Tibetan Buddhist meditation involves keeping your eyes slightly open while meditating, to keep the mind mildly conscious. This is the same effect we're trying to achieve with the current meditation process. Sometimes, I like to meditate with my eyes open and focus on a single object, usually the flame of a candle. Similar to listening to constant and consistent sounds around you, focussing on something relatively still and unchanging, like a candle or any other material object, works equally well in helping you enter a deep meditative state.

## 4. Try Active Meditation

Although my preferred way to meditate is seated, it needn't be so for you. Active meditation may involve exercise or walking. Leverage the time you spend at the gym, or during your own workout at home, to meditate. Rather than distracting yourself by watching TV or chatting to a friend on the phone, focus on something static in your environment, or just focus on the exercise you're doing. This still gives your mind something to think about, distracting it from its limiting chatter.

Yoga is a wonderful practice of active meditation, as the various poses invite Source Energy to move through you. By focussing on each pose that you practice – how your body responds to it and how you feel while practicing it – you not only accomplish the almost thoughtless state we've talked about, but you also amplify the effectiveness of the poses and allow Source Energy to saturate your physical body, too.

## Consistency is Key

Meditation is one of the most powerful processes in nurturing your light, but it'll only work if you practice it consistently. The easiest way to do it is by adding it to your daily spiritual practice, so that it becomes a daily habit. Having meditated for over 10 years, I can confidently say that meditation is the number one tool that led me to finding and following my purpose, and I'm certain that it'll help you do the same.

In time, as you practice being in the receptive mode that meditation makes available, you'll feel your capacity to hold light expand. As you consistently tune your mind and body to the vibration of your inner being, and strengthen your happiness muscles, you'll find yourself becoming more resilient in the face of life's daily struggles. Things that bothered you will seem petty and insignificant, and people that angered you will become irrelevant, as you'll be so accustomed to feeling good that nothing else will matter.

# Chapter 16

# PARTNERING WITH THE ELEMENTALS

My high school Geography teacher always used to tell me, 'It's not about saving Planet Earth, it's about saving the human race,' and I agree with her.

The earth, our great mother, has been through it all and has always come out the winner. She's survived billions of years of environmental destructions and catastrophes, and she's always managed to find her balance again. What didn't survive were the civilisations that attempted to mess up her balance, abuse her and claim her as their own.

One thing that my Geography degree made clear to me is that the earth has powerful systems and processes in place for detoxifying all forms of external impurity. The wind processes, ocean currents, volcanoes and plate tectonics all work in unison to filter out what interferes with the natural flow of things. If we're not careful, they'll filter us out, too.

From a spiritual perspective, the earth has a spirit and consciousness in the same way that we do. Every single piece of consciousness in the natural world is a portal of pure-positive Source Energy. Plants, flowers, trees, rocks, rivers, the sea and the wind possess spirit, energy, consciousness and beingness, just like we do. Collectively, the spirits and beings of nature are known as the elementals.

The elementals of earth, air, water, fire and spirit are the intelligence behind the thriving and functioning of our planet. They work both individually and collectively to not only ensure the natural functioning of our planet, but also to help us flow and thrive in the same way that nature does. We are part of nature, too, after all.

The elementals care about us staying here. Haven't you noticed the recent popularity of mermaids, fairies and unicorns in spirituality as well as popular culture? The reason for these nature spirits popping up into our consciousness more frequently is because they're actively trying to catch our attention. They realise that we've gone astray recently, particularly in regard to how we've been treating the planet, and they want to point us back in the right direction.

The elementals are extending an olive branch, so that we can work together and remember how to flow and thrive alongside nature in every area of our lives, and especially in relation to the planet.

## Nurturing Your Light in Nature

Spending time in nature is the easiest and fastest way to nurture your light and tune yourself to your inner being. As I mentioned earlier, every single piece of consciousness in the natural world is a portal of Source Energy. When you step into nature, you allow the all-powerful, pure-positive aura of nature to envelop you, as the elementals work in clearing your physical, emotional and mental bodies, restoring you back to your 'factory settings.'

Although a simple nature walk will work wonders in clearing you and helping to nurture light, connecting with specific elemental beings can help you find balance in specific life areas.

There are five types of elementals:

1. **Earth** elementals guide your relationship with the physical world, such as money, your home, your body and your sense of protection, safety and security. They are excellent at helping you manifest an abundance of material possessions, as well as feel grounded in your human body and life on earth. Earth elementals are collectively known as gnomes or faeries, and these also include tree dryads, woodland nymphs, mountain giants and flower fairies, among many others.

2. **Air** elementals govern your thoughts and beliefs, including past life beliefs. They help clear your mind of belief systems that don't serve you, creating space for divine guidance to flow through. They work well with fire elementals to help clear stress and help you find a state of peace. Air elementals are collectively known as sylphs, and these also include the four winds and various breeze spirits.

3. **Water** elementals oversee your relationships, emotions and sexuality. They embody the Divine Feminine, and help you to navigate your emotional world. They're relationship experts, showing you how to safely deal with suppressed emotions, share vulnerabilities and manifest fulfilling relationships. Water elementals are collectively known as undines, and these also include the ocean, lake and river mermaids, along with water nymphs and sprites.

4. **Fire** elementals govern the realms of change, manifestation, motivation, transformation and purification. They embody the Divine Masculine and inspire within you the courage you need to take action towards your dreams, desires and life purpose. Fire elementals are collectively known as the dragons, and these include salamanders, the phoenix, the earth core and volcano dragons, as well as various sun dragons.

5. **Spirit** elementals oversee your soul path, life purpose and career choices. They embody the spirit of your soul and bring forth your authenticity and divine knowledge. They know exactly what it takes to find, follow and fulfil your life purpose. They also work with all other elementals to help them channel Source Energy through their various functions. Spirit elementals include unicorns, pegasians and the muses.

## Nurturing Your Light with the Elementals

All consistent interaction with the natural world will help nurture your inner love and light, but consciously interacting with the elements and elementals will help nurture your light in specific life areas. Ensuring that your light flows in every area of your life is important for your consistent connection to Source and overall wellbeing.

Think of an imbalanced life area as a virus that, if left unattended, will eventually and progressively infect other areas of your life, blocking the flow of your light as a whole. Balancing the flow of light in each and every area of your life ensures that your well of love and light isn't *leaking*. It keeps it full, so that you can work it in following your purpose.

## Meditation to Meet Your Elemental Guides

Use the following meditation to connect to the five elemental types mentioned above, to balance specific blocks and life areas that require your attention:

1. Identify a concern, frustration, obstacle or an area of your life that's currently blocked.

2. Consult the elemental list above to figure out the type of element and its elementals that can help you balance this. Use your intuition to pick a specific elemental to work with. It's usually the first one that stands out.

3. Either physically or in meditation, go somewhere you can access that element. You could go to a park (earth), the beach (water), a mountain (air), near a bonfire or candle (fire) or your meditation space (spirit).

4. Sit in meditation at that physical or virtual place, and allow yourself to experience that element with all your senses. Smell the fresh grass, feel the warmth of the sun on your face, touch the earth beneath you and taste the air. Immerse yourself in the energy of the element surrounding you.

5. Thinking about your concern, or the ways that things aren't working out in that specific life area, call upon your chosen elemental and ask them to make themselves present. You may see, feel or hear them, or just know when they're there with you.

6. Ask your elemental guide to help balance your specific concern, and then observe as they take an energetic healing ball and place it gently within your heart. The light from the energetic ball expands through your body and outwards into the affected area, whether it's caused by a concern, a block or a life area in general, touching all people involved and restoring the balance. Stay in this state for as long as it feels good to do so.

7. When the process feels complete, thank your elemental guide and come out of meditation,

knowing that they will always be with you, guiding the positive changes that'll come.

You can download an expanded audio recording of this meditation at GeorgeLizos.com/LGW

This healing meditation will resolve whatever situation you may be going through on an energetic level. In the days and weeks that follow, you will receive intuitive guidance on making changes that'll allow you to actualise the changes in a physical way. The Universe will also support the process by rearranging people, experiences and circumstances to help restore the balance.

# Chapter 17

# BATHING IN SUNLIGHT, MOONLIGHT AND STARLIGHT

By my fifth year living in the UK, I'd found myself feeling incredibly lethargic, even mildly depressed. I was conscious that my workaholic lifestyle was unsustainable, but even in the moments where I'd spend time out in nature relaxing, I'd feel less joyful than usual. Asking my guides about it, they said something I didn't expect:

*'The external light from the sun, moon and stars reflects your inner light. As you've chronically deprived yourself of natural external light, you've limited your ability to nurture your inner light.'*

Although I'd been aware of the scientific reasoning behind the positive impact that sunlight has on our physical, emotional and mental health, I'd never thought about it from a spiritual perspective. Neither had I thought about the role that the stars and moon play in all of this.

In the following three years, under the guidance of the elementals, I explored the healing benefits of these types of natural, cosmic lights. I'd grab any opportunity I had to meditate under the stars, the moon and the sun, receiving guidance from them and comparing the impact they had on my energy.

Before we explore these different cosmic lights, it's important to remember that although external light can help nurture your inner light, you don't really need it to do so. *You* have all the power and skills you need to nurture all aspects of your inner light. Working with the tools that nature has given us simply makes the process easier.

## Sunlight

Tuning into the energy of the sun, I encountered Helios, the Greek God, as well as his three groups of dragons, the morning, midday and sunset dragons.

Helios imparted that he not only personifies the physical sun, but also the spiritual aspect of the sun that holds the same vibration as our soul. In the same way that the sun is in the centre of our solar system, upon which myriad planets and stars depend for nurturance, so is our soul the centre of our being. Meditating or bathing under the sunlight in safe and healthy increments is a powerful way to use its external light to switch on our soul's internal light.

Although we don't need sunlight to tune ourselves to the vibration of our souls, exposing ourselves to it makes the tuning in process easier.

Exposing ourselves to the morning, midday or evening sunlight has different effects on us. The morning sunlight, carried by the morning dragons, is a great motivator. It holds a kickstarting vibration that motivates us to get started with our day and start working towards our life purpose. It embodies the Divine Masculine, and inspires within our souls the desire to make stuff happen.

The midday sunlight, carried by the midday dragons, has a cleansing and transformative kind of energy. That's when the sun is at its strongest, and exposing ourselves to small increments of this sunlight is a great way to clear our aura of any negative vibrations that we've taken on during the day – e.g. negative cords of attachment to people, things, and projects – and get a quick vibrational fix before we proceed with the rest of our day.

The evening sunlight, carried by the sunset dragons, holds the feminine side of the Divine Masculine. It may sound paradoxical, but these dragons remind us that resting is as productive as taking action. They encourage us to cease action, take a break and be mindful of the divine guidance for action, which must flow through as a result.

The three phases of the sun each light up a different side of our soul, keeping us focussed on following our life purpose in a balanced way that doesn't deplete us.

## Starlight

Starlight, on the other hand, has a purely feminine energy. Unlike the motivating qualities of the sun, the soft, trembling, almost timid white light that the stars emit speak to the receptive qualities of our soul. Our soul is perfectly balanced in masculine and feminine energy, and while the sun activates the masculine, action-taking aspect of it, the stars activate the feminine, surrendering aspect of who we are. Both are needed to be fully aligned to Source, and therefore to follow our life purpose.

There aren't many words to describe the healing effects of starlight, merely because its very functions involve ceasing thinking, not using our logic and letting go of the need to explain things, in order to allow ourselves to just be. Starlight reminds us that life, like nature, isn't just about creating and taking action, and that being totally still and inactive is also important.

Bathing under starlight will help you get into a deep meditative state fast, allowing you to release resistance and receive answers to questions that you've had and find solutions to problems that you've struggled with. This receptive state also gets you in touch with your emotions and vulnerability, encouraging you to release suppressed emotions, feel things fully and find the courage to deal with deep emotional wounds.

Starlight is most potent during the dark or new moon phases, when their light is strongest and unaffected by the light of the moon. It's also a good idea to bathe under starlight somewhere in nature, where there isn't much artificial light from houses or streetlamps. I've had my most powerful experiences with starlight while meditating on the beach or sleeping outside of my mountain country house.

## Moonlight

Although traditionally the moon is associated with the Divine Feminine, while connecting with it during meditation, I learned that it actually strikes a balance between the feminine and the masculine. Moonlight is created when the dark and feminine energy of the moon interacts with the bright and masculine energy of the sun. Thus, moonlight combines both energies, and when taken in consistent increments, it acts as a great spiritual vitamin for manifestation.

Have you noticed that the full moon usually makes you feel overwhelmed and uneasy? I believe that the reason for this has less to do with full moon energy as such, and is more about us not exposing ourselves to moonlight throughout the entire moon cycle. In ancient times, when people lived rural lives and were more connected to the cycles of nature, they honoured the moon in all its phases. Nowadays, people seldom honour the moon at all, and the ones who do only do so during the new and full moon phases.

By losing touch with the moon and its phases, we've lost touch with the moonlight's healing qualities, too. So, when we get out to admire the full moon once a month, we get hit by an overwhelming wave of energy that throws us off balance.

Moonlight is best received in small increments of at least ten minutes every evening for the duration of its cycle. Its light has jolting and motivating qualities, combining the action-oriented, creative energy of the sun with the surrendering, receptive energy of the moon to jolt our energy. It pushes us out of our comfort zone, causing us to rethink our choices, take risks and add some spice to the way we live our life and follow our purpose.

Without moonlight, life would be boring. You'd be waking up in the morning, keeping yourself busy with unimportant tasks during the day, going to sleep and then repeating the following day. There wouldn't be any contrast or unforeseen circumstances, and there'd be no desire to break the stereotypes and create something totally new. You'd still be growing, but in far slower degree than you would with moonlight's motivating qualities.

## How to Bathe in Sunlight, Starlight and Moonlight

Depending on the qualities that are currently missing from your life, choose one of the three types of light that you need the most. Then, follow the steps in this process to bathe under your chosen light for at least 30 days:

1. Choose a spot out in nature to bathe under your chosen light. It's better to choose a quiet place away from distractions, where you can be alone.

2. Sit or lay down on the ground, or anywhere you feel most comfortable, and come into a meditative state. Gradually relax your muscles and let yourself be in the present moment.

3. Mentally ask the light from the sun, stars or moon above to work their magic on you. Ask for the spirit or consciousness of them to come forth and connect with you. You may feel as though the sun's dragons are coming forth, or any other spirits, gods, goddesses and elementals that you need to connect with at that moment in time.

4. Rather than trying to control the process, let the spirits that come forth, or simply the light you're exposed to, do their work. They may choose to have a conversation, perform healing or just simply hold space for the healing or activation to take place. Go with what comes up, and remember that you can't get it wrong. Simply exposing yourself to the light creates the change that you need within you.

5. Stay there for at least ten minutes, and once you're done, thank the spirit(s) that you've come into contact with and come out of meditation.

Chapter 18

# PLACES OF POWER

Aside from utilising external sources of physical light from the sun, stars and moon to tune into and nurture your inner light, you can also utilise the spiritual light and energy in what I call places of power.

I remember learning about the creation of sacred space as part of my degree in Geography. My professor introduced the three main theories concerning the matter:

## 1. Sacred Space is an Ontological Given

This first theory suggests that sacred space exists naturally in various naturally spiritual or high-vibrational places around the world. The town of Glastonbury in the UK is such a space, where the convergence of the Mary and Michael ley lines create a naturally high-vibe and sacred space.

Although the term 'ley line' was first coined by Alfred Watkins in 1921, the theory of a planetary energy grid has existed since ancient times. In 360 BC, the Greek philosopher Plato proposed that the base structure of our planet evolved geometrically in five shapes, today known as the Platonic Solids. The result is a geometric energy grid superimposed on, and forming the energetic basis of, the earth. According to Plato, this energy literally holds the earth together.

When two or more of these energetic lines converge, they create what I call natural places of power, which act as portals of Source Energy that bridge the celestial and physical planes. Many well-known sacred sites around the world are located at such crossroads, including the Glastonbury Tor, Stonehenge, the Pyramids at Giza, Mount Shasta and Machu Picchu.

## 2.  Sacred Space is a Social Construct

The second theory puts forward the idea that sacred space is created when a group of people perform regular sacred practices long enough that a non-ontologically sacred space becomes sacred.

The Camino de Santiago pilgrimage in Spain could be seen as such a kind of a sacred space. Although there's nothing to single it out as a naturally sacred space, the thousands of people who do the pilgrimage every year have given the space its sacredness. Group meditation, yoga, tai chi or any other spiritual practice in your local gym or park are also examples of this theory. Whenever a group of people come together consistently to carry out a spiritual practice, they inadvertently project their collective sacred energy onto the surrounding space, making it sacred, too.

## 3.  Sacred Space is a Mental Construct

The third theory surrounding sacred space is the one that you're probably most familiar with already, as you prove it to yourself each time you meditate, pray, do a full moon ritual or any other form of solitary spiritual practice. This theory suggests that we can all create our own personal sacred space around our physical bodies using focus and intention.

In practical terms, whenever you meditate, your vibration raises and extends to the space around you, rendering it sacred. In other words, according to this theory, sacred space is personal and portable and can be created anywhere, anytime, as long as you focus your intention in aligning with your inner being.

Which of these theories do you think is the correct one? How is sacred space created? Does it simply exist, do we create it in groups or do we create it with our own personal intention?

Personally, I believe that all three theories are valid, and when used intentionally and in combination, we can create powerful sacred spaces that act as a source of replenishing and nurturing for our inner light.

## Portals of Light

When you use any one of these processes, or a combination of them, consciously and with intention, you can create an extra-potent sacred space that I call a portal of light. This is a physical space that you transform into a sacred energy temple, a bridge between heaven and earth, which you can access physically or virtually for weeks, months or even years after its creation. You can visit this portal whenever you want to replenish your inner light and reconnect to your inner being.

Picture this:

*You're sitting at the top of the Glastonbury Tor, a sacred mountain through which the Michael and Mary ley lines cross, bringing forth the balance of the Divine Masculine and Divine Feminine. You're sitting there, eyes closed, in deep meditation; so deep that you feel like you're floating. Your aura expands in the space around you, your whole body is vibrating with love and happiness and you're filled with light.*

*Your friends join you in a circle. Following your lead, they close their eyes and go into deep meditation, too. There's a sudden rise in the temperature around you, as their expanding auras merge with yours and one another's. Your respective sacred spaces blend, and together with the naturally high-vibrating energy of the Tor, you create what feels like heaven on Earth. You're in utter bliss, all of you.*

*When you finally come out of meditation, you all feel elated – lit up!*

Taking the time to visit a naturally occurring place of power, and consciously adding to its sacredness by using the other two practices, is a sure way to create a portal of light. You can access this each time you meditate, either by visualising yourself being there, or making annual trips to the space to access the energy in a more physical way. For years, Glastonbury has been my portal of light, and if it wasn't for my annual summer trip there to fuel me, I'd still be totally burnt out and depleted.

Although combining all three processes of creating sacred space is the ideal way of opening a portal of light, you can open one using two or even just one of these processes. Remember, Source and your guides want to connect with you. They're not withholding their love and light; they share it easily and plentifully. All you need to do is set your intention to opening a portal of light, and then use any of these processes to make it happen.

## Opening a Portal of Light

To open your personal portal of light within a physical space, follow these steps:

1. Begin by choosing which of the three processes of sacred space creation you'd like to utilise. These include visiting a naturally occurring place of power, carrying out a spiritual activity with a group of people or doing so in a solitary manner.

2. Choose the physical space you'd like to open a portal of light in. This could be an ontologically sacred space, somewhere in your house – such as your altar space – or any other easily accessible physical space. Ideally, choose somewhere you love being.

3. Whether you're with a group of people or by yourself, sit comfortably somewhere you feel safe and close your eyes, coming into meditation.

4. Imagine that there's an energetic line extending from your root chakra at the base of your spine, digging deep into the earth. It passes through layers of soil, rock and crystal caves, down through the earth's magma, tying itself around the earth's core. Ground yourself to the powerhouse of our planet and establish your connection with it. Feel its subtle energy gently cleansing and recalibrating your own.

5. Now, let an energetic line extend from your crown chakra at the top of your head up into the sky. Let it meet with something that represents Source, be it a god, goddess or the Universe, and make a connection to it. Feel yourself opening up to the possibilities that exist beyond your physicality, and let Source's light fill you up and inspire you.

6. Having connected to heaven and earth, you're now ready to connect the two and open a portal of light on the physical space you're in. Visualise a spiralling vortex of light birthing from the base of the Earth's core and growing upwards through your energetic connection to it, into your physical body and up into the sky. Let this vortex grow bigger and stronger with each breath that you take.

7. Set your intention that this vortex of pure-positive Source energy stays there forever, or for as long as

you need it, so that you can access it physically or virtually at any time.

8. With gratitude, come out of meditation and open your eyes.

## Opening a Virtual Portal of Light

How did you feel after reading through and visualising the Glastonbury Tor meditation scenario earlier? Didn't you feel more lit up than you did before reading it? Do you really need to be on that Tor, meditating with a group of friends, to get that high on light?

Not really. Portals of light can be created both physically and virtually. Sure, travelling to Glastonbury, visiting ancient temples, meditating in groups or going on a pilgrimage is the preferred way to open a portal of light, but you can also do so in a virtual way.

Follow the following meditation to open a virtual portal of light in a physical space you're not currently occupying, which you can go to for the purpose of replenishing or nurturing your light whenever you need to:

1. Pick a physical, naturally sacred space (or not) that you feel drawn to.

2. In meditation, visualise yourself sitting in meditation in that space. Allow yourself to experience it with all your senses, and ask the spirits of the space to make themselves present and help you to open a portal of light.

112

3. Visualise a group of friends, your guides or angels, or even complete strangers who you feel an affinity with, sitting in meditation with you. Feel their energy around you and notice how your aura interacts with theirs. Clear your mind of thought as much as possible, allowing your energy to naturally rise. Your friends are doing the same.

4. Together, follow steps four to seven from the 'Opening a Portal of Light' meditation to open the virtual portal of light.

5. Bask in the energy of that light. Let it recalibrate and uplift you. Register the feeling of it, and know that you can access it whenever you want in your meditations.

6. When you feel ready, come out of meditation feeling uplifted.

# Chapter 19

# FINDING YOUR TRIBE

Our light is best nurtured when we share it with people who get, understand and support us. We're social beings, and it is in our nature to cluster together in groups of people with whom we share common interests, viewpoints, lifestyles and characteristics. Although we feel comfortable doing that with our hobbies and political choices, we're apprehensive about doing so with our spiritual beliefs.

How can we trust others with our spiritual beliefs or interests, when doing so has resulted in us being persecuted and killed in past lives? How can we feel safe in sharing our innermost fears with one another, when our sisters and brothers stabbed us in the back during the witch trials of the 16th and 17th centuries? Even after we've healed these past wounds and expectations, how can we share our diverse spiritual beliefs in a Christian world that sees things in black and white, good or evil?

As a result, we believe that it's us against the world and we can't trust anyone. People are out to get us, and the only person we should depend on is ourselves.

Yet, we long for connectedness, intimacy, partnership and sisterhood. We long to belong to a group of people who genuinely care about us, share our beliefs, will help us get

114

up on our feet when we fall and encourage us to keep moving forward when we succeed.

I believe that the importance of finding our tribe is underrated. Being connected to people and the world around us is inherent to who we are. Remember, we're all made out of love and light, and are connected in a giant energetic web of consciousness. We're intrinsically interconnected to the people around us, and keeping ourselves from creating strong connections for fear of being hurt or betrayed inadvertently puts a cap on the amount of light we can nurture, or allow to flow through us at all times.

We can achieve a lot just by ourselves, but to create big change in the world, we have to go about it together.

## I Can Do it Better Alone

Growing up, I used to hate being or working with other people. At school, whenever we were assigned a group project, I'd go up to the teacher and ask if I could do it by myself. I believed I was better than everyone else, and that going about it with others would simply slow me down. Sadly, the teacher always accepted.

As a result, I grew up not having friends, being unable to work in a group and arrogantly refusing to interact with other people altogether. Although I felt safe in my independence, I also felt miserable, alone and unworthy. As much as I tried to be satisfied by just being me, I lacked the sense of support, comradeship and community that bonding with others provides.

It wasn't until I was encouraged to work with other people later on, while at university, that I allowed myself to experience the benefits of being part of a tribe or community.

## Overcoming the Fear of Connection

How do we go about overcoming our fear of connecting with other people, and subsequently finding our tribe?

In my experience, connection became easier if I started with a single person. I met my best friend during the summer holidays at the age of 15. We bonded over our love of Harry Potter, crystals and incense sticks. We'd spend our weekends visiting the local crystal shop, chatting about dream interpretation and attending astral projection workshops. It wasn't easy for either of us to trust the other, but we understood that trust came with time, experiences shared and from being vulnerable with each other.

We gradually opened up to each other about our fears, concerns and frustrations. Bit by bit, chat after chat, our vulnerability nurtured trust. As this process unfolded, the trust we built replaced our fear of betrayal or persecution. Suddenly, we found ourselves telling a different story about people, intimacy and connection.

We find our tribe when we realise that we can't find an answer to a problem by trying to get to the bottom of it. This is true with everything in life. The more we try to resolve a problem, the bigger it gets, and we keep recreating it with our experiences. The only way to find an answer to a problem is by focussing on, thinking about and practicing the solution to it. In other words, the only way to get out of a negative situation is by living a positive one.

Therefore, when it comes to finding your tribe, start practicing the solution to your problem by opening up to a single person. As you connect, share and trust, you nurture the energy of your desired reality. You set up your first tribe, and even if it consists of just the two of you to begin with, eventually it'll grow. It *must* grow, for that which you put your attention towards always does. In time, the Universe will knock itself out to orchestrate rendezvous with people, online or offline, to give you more of what you've asked for.

## Online Tribes

Although the idea of being physically connected to, and hanging out with, a group of people we share similar spiritual beliefs with is what we expect, it's important to be open to new avenues and platforms of spiritual tribes.

The world is constantly changing, and if we don't change with it, we'll simply limit our opportunities for being part of a community. That's why I'm a big supporter of online communities. Personally, my spiritual tribe is almost 100% online, not because I don't enjoy hanging out in real life, but because I enjoy hanging out virtually more.

You may be different, and that's OK. If you've already found your in-person tribe, well done. Keep on loving, supporting and growing with them. However, if you long for an in-person tribe, but are struggling to find people who you match with where you live, or you simply enjoy hanging out online more, give yourself permission to start looking for your tribe online.

In our technologically advanced and interconnected world, it's become incredibly easy to hang out online. There's a Facebook group community for every possible spiritual modality, religion, interest or belief system, and easy ways to communicate with one another via text, audio and video. I have two such communities, both of which welcome people of all spiritual beliefs.

My first Facebook group community, *Your Spiritual Toolkit*, is like a virtual Hogwarts, where spiritual seekers come to support and be supported, as well as to share spiritual tools and guidance that'll empower us to follow our life purpose. *Elemental Communication* is my second community, with fellow author Calista, focussed on partnering with the elementals of earth, air, water, fire and spirit. I look forward to welcoming you into both communities if these are topics that resonate with you.

If not, what do you believe in? What do you seek in a spiritual tribe? How do you want it to feel while being part of it?

Search for it on Facebook, and then join the communities that feel right to you. Use your emotions for guidance, hang out in a few groups, interact with people and see where you feel most at home. You'd be surprised to find out how strong a connection you can make with people online. In time, you'll find yourself texting, voice messaging, video chatting and even arranging to meet and hang out in real life. Remember, it only takes one person to find your tribe. Start there, and let the Universe do the rest.

# Chapter 20

# COMING OUT OF THE SPIRITUAL CLOSET

Growing up, I got comfortable living in closets. From a young age, the world had told me that to be worthy and accepted, I had to be a certain way. Anything and everything that didn't fit into what's accepted had to be suppressed. So, I got really good at hiding these 'unacceptable' aspects of myself. Mentally and emotionally, I created virtual compartments that I'd use to hide the aspects of myself that didn't fit into the stereotypes that people wanted me to conform to.

We all do this in one way or another. Our shadow self includes the parts of us that have been rejected or shamed at some point in our lives, either by others or by ourselves. Rather than dealing with the emotion of shame and bringing these aspects of our personality into the light for healing, we often choose to hide them. It's the easy way out. People didn't like those aspects of us anyway; they made them uncomfortable, and it made us uncomfortable to see them uncomfortable. They threatened our sense of belonging in the world, so why suddenly bring them out of the darkness they've become so accustomed to?

Although hiding the shadow self from the world and ourselves keeps it from expressing itself, it is still an active and alive part of us, and that won't stop being the case. Hiding it only strengthens its desire to be freed until, in time, it will increasingly demand our attention. Its voice will grow louder, begging us to let its freak flag fly. We can resist it for as long as possible, but it will eventually get the better of us. In a moment of weakness, it'll burst out of its dark prison and take over, and what could've been a quiet time at home dealing with uncomfortable emotions is now a raging monster, wreaking havoc in our lives.

## Lightworkers' Collective Shadow

For many lightworkers, our spiritual beliefs are part of our shadow self. Having spent lifetimes being judged, shamed, persecuted and killed simply for being ourselves, we came into this lifetime with an expectation of being rejected by others and the world at large. Even if we hadn't personally experienced persecution in our past lives, our connectedness to one another as a result of our soul realms and our collective lightworker soul makes us vulnerable to the past life experiences of the whole.

As a result of our collective expectation for persecution, we manifest judgement and rejection early on in our lives that holds us hostage throughout our adult years. In my case, as a result of being rejected in past lives for being a witch, a healer and a priest, I manifested bullying early on in this life because, on a soul level, I had an expectation for rejection. Even though I've found self-empowerment through these childhood experiences and haven't felt bullied in years now, I still expect it. Whenever I meet someone new, I expect attack. I expect them to judge me, think I'm weird, reject and make fun of me.

Despite all the work I've done to release this expectation, it still remains active within me, and it'll probably stay active to some degree for years to come.

How, then, do we go about healing our shadow selves and vacating the spiritual closet once and for all?

## If You Can't Beat Fear, Just Do it Scared

I like to think of a lightworker's spiritual closet as a maze of closets that we need to come out of. There is the closet of coming to terms with our own spiritual beliefs; the closet of sharing our spirituality with our friends, family and loved ones; and the closet of sharing our spirituality with the world, among others.

There isn't a cookie-cutter formula for coming out of our spiritual closets. The truth is, it's scary as fuck. I'm not going to sugar-coat it for you; the judgment that you fear may actually come; the friends that you fear you will lose may really leave; the life that you fear will change will indeed change in more ways that you can imagine.

So, the question that naturally comes to mind is, why come out in the first place?

The answer may be tough to hear, but it's also necessary. As a lightworker, coming out of your spiritual closets has less to do with your comfort zone and more to do with the people you're here to serve, the message you're here to teach and the change you're here to create. In other words, your life purpose has more to do with the collective whole rather than just with you.

From this perspective, are you willing to withhold your wisdom, guidance and light from the people you're here to serve? Are you really prepared to slow down the ascension of the planet because you're scared of your life changing? Do you really want to play it safe and stay in your comfort zone when you know that your purpose could help create real, powerful changes in the world?

It's time for you to truly rise up, lightworker. It's time to rise up to who you are and to what living your purpose means. Doing so involves coming out of your spiritual closets unapologetically, even if that will bring about messy life changes and uncomfortable emotions. You owe it to the people you're here to serve, to all of us, and to the world.

Staying in your spiritual closets puts a cap on the amount of light you can nurture and express in the world. In other words, how can you truly work your light when you're not letting it shine fully? Imagine you're taking the brightest lamp, placing it inside a box and then putting the box in a dark room and expecting it to light the place up. That's what you're doing when you stay within the spiritual closets.

## How to Come Out

As I mentioned earlier, there's no cookie-cutter formula for coming out of the spiritual closets, but there are guidelines you can follow.

In my experience, the easiest way to heal your fears of change and persecution that coming out of your spiritual closet brings up is to embrace them. In other words, the only way to overcome something you're fearful of is by doing it, because once you've done it, there's nothing left to fear. Most importantly, when you're ready and willing to heal your fears, the Universe will come in to provide additional support.

Here's how it works:

1. With each spiritual closet you come out of, you expand the amount of love and light that your being can hold. Coming out of a spiritual closet is equivalent to accepting more of who you are and releasing the judgement and shame that you've previously held towards yourself. Since who you are is love and light, accepting more of yourself equates to accepting more love and light flowing through you.

2. It is this light that will sustain you through the changes that'll come as a result of coming out of the closet. It is this light that will comfort you when certain family members reject you, and also help you to heal those relationships. It is this light that

124

will comfort you when friends leave your life, giving you the courage to replace them with new ones. It is this light that will support you when your entire life shifts in a different direction, helping you to stand back up on your feet.

Therefore, although coming out of your spiritual closets may initially be uncomfortable, it'll also bring possibilities for comfort that you've never imagined.

3. Not only will the love and light you'll nurture as a result support you through these changes, but the Universe will show up to support you, too. When you show up for you by fully accepting who you are, the Universe will show up for you by orchestrating the perfect set of circumstances to go through these changes as effortlessly as possible. Acceptance of the self is the greatest way of showing up for you, and it must be met by the Universe's greatest effort in doing the same for you, too.

# PART III

# WORK YOUR LIGHT

# Chapter 21

# LIGHTWORK VS. EGOWORK

Taking action comes from either a place of light or a place of ego. When your action is inspired from a state of being in alignment with your light, and therefore your inner being, it is divinely guided. If, on the other hand, your action comes from a state of being in discord with your inner being, it is ego guidance.

So far in this book, you've defined your life purpose and then used a variety of tools and processes to nurture your connection to your light and inner being. The aim of the third part of the book is to introduce ways that you can leverage your connectedness to follow your purpose and create positive change in the world.

Rather than guiding you to take specific action relating to your purpose, I'll instead share my top manifestation processes and guidance points to help inspire the action steps within you, and to also leverage the Universe's support as you move forward. You'll also learn how to deepen your connection to your spirit guides, so that you receive clearer guidance.

However, before we get started, it's important to preface this part with the distinction between lightwork and egowork, so that you can unequivocally know whether the guidance you receive at any point is coming from your inner being or from your disconnection from it.

## Programmed to Exhaustion

If there's one thing I learned during my burnout years, it's that patriarchy is deeply embedded in our world and our psyches. Even after I'd done a lot of work healing and embracing my feminine energy, my masculine imbalance persisted in covert, subtle ways long after. It wasn't until I worked with past life regression that I was able to bring it to the light and heal it completely.

From the moment we enter this world, we're programmed to think in a masculine way: go to school, get the grades, get into university and get a good job. We're given a blueprint of how our lives should be, and there's barely any feminine energy in that blueprint. It's all focussed on mindless hustle, putting ourselves into limiting boxes and following stereotypical formulas for success.

No one teaches us how to be happy or to follow our intuition. We're not taught to meditate before making important decisions, or how to align to our inner being before choosing the direction we want to take in life.

As a result, when I ask you to take action towards following your life purpose, chances are that you'll go about it in a purely masculine way. You'll most probably use what you've learnt so far to go about it. You'll set your goals, make a plan and start taking action.

.

Don't do that; let's take a different approach. Your wholly masculine way of taking action is only contributing to the patriarchal paradigm we're working to untangle. Finding balance requires a feminine way of using masculine energy.

## Taking Inspired Action

Ultimately, masculine energy and feminine energy are just labels we've created to help understand ourselves and the world we live in. In truth, when we find alignment with our inner beings, we're innately balanced in masculine and feminine energy, and we don't need to micromanage ourselves or the ways in which we use these energies.

There's a feminine way to be masculine, i.e. to take action, and there's a masculine way to be feminine, i.e. to chill out. There's an innate balance within each of these states that, when found, ensures that we use these energies in a constructive rather than a destructive way. True balance is only achieved when, no matter the energy we're leveraging at any point, we're concurrently leveraging its 'opposing' energy, too.

In practical terms, following our masculine energy in a feminine way has to do with taking inspired (lightwork) rather than forced (egowork) action. Forced action is our default, indoctrinated state. It's what we're programmed to do in this patriarchal world. It's meaningless action that has no love and light backing it up. It's rooted in our ego's capabilities, rather than our inner being's. It's a limited way of taking action because it only leverages one side of us, the physical one.

Inspired action, on the other hand, is divinely guided. It comes after we've taken the time to nurture our light consistently, and is informed not by our ego, but also by our inner being and our connectedness to the Universe. Inspired action feels exciting and unequivocal. There's no doubt as to whether it's true or not. It feels real and certain, because it really is.

When people ask me what the difference is between ego and divine guidance, my answer is simple: when it's divine guidance, you've already followed it. When it's divine guidance, you know it's true. Your entire being affirms and knows its validity. It always comes from a place of feeling happy and loving, and for this reason, you've already taken steps towards it.

Ego guidance feels unsure. You doubt it, and you doubt yourself over it; you ask other people's opinions about it; you weigh the pros and cons and play out future scenarios in your mind. It comes from a place of fear rather than love, and you feel that emotion.

## Working Your Light

As you try out the processes and exercises in the following chapters, keep the distinction between lightwork and egowork in mind. Although you've consistently nurtured your light throughout the previous section of the book, take time to get into a lit-up state before trying out the manifestation and psychic processes to come. This will ensure that the guidance for action that comes through is inspired from your light rather than your ego, and that you're on the right track to following your life purpose.

# Chapter 22

# THE SECRET BEHIND THE SECRET

In 2006, the movie *The Secret* sent millions of people thinking their thoughts into reality, or so they thought. Now, I'm not here to bash *The Secret*, since it was also my entry into the Law of Attraction and manifestation. The movie and the book that followed raised collective consciousness significantly, as they introduced the idea of consciously creating our lives to the masses.

However, *The Secret* didn't really share the actual secret of the Law of Attraction, as mass consciousness wasn't ready for it at the time. According to *The Secret*, and most of the other manifestation books out there, our thoughts create our reality. This isn't entirely true, though, and this is where the real secret lies.

Our thoughts don't create our reality, our emotions do. Our thoughts are simply the creators of our emotions, and therefore of our vibrational frequency.

As we already established earlier in this book, we're made out of love and light. Therefore, we're energy – vibration, and the degree to which our vibrational frequency varies depends on the degree to which we're aligned to our light.

When we're fully aligned to our light, and therefore feel the emotions of love and happiness, our vibrational frequency is high. Likewise, when we're disconnected from our light, and feel emotions such as depression and despair, our vibrational frequency is low.

The Universe responds to the vibrational frequency we emit, rather than the thoughts we think or the words we speak. Our thoughts and words, then, are merely tools that we use to shift our emotions, and therefore our vibration.

## Ego vs. Light-Driven Manifestation

The reason why the distinction between our thoughts and emotions is so important to make is because attempting to manifest by micromanaging our thoughts can easily send us down the ego path of manifestation. When we exclude emotion from the equation, we can get caught up in a superficial cycle of doing affirmations and thinking positive thoughts for the sake of manifesting the desires that our ego thinks will make us happy.

Instead, when we do the emotional work first and bring ourselves into alignment with our light, the desires inspired from this state are always aligned with our life purpose and soul callings.

Furthermore, when we approach manifestation from an emotional standpoint, we stop seeing the Universe as a power outside of us that we demand things from, and instead see it as a collaborator. We realise that we're not here to will the Universe to do our bidding, we're here to

134

discover our role in the process and collaborate with the Universe in order to bring about the creation of our desires and purpose.

Getting lit up before attempting conscious manifestation transforms the way that we perceive ourselves in relation to the Universe, which ultimately results in more effortless and fulfilling manifestation.

# Chapter 23

# YOUR VIBRATIONAL SAFE

Are you a conscious or an unconscious manifestor?

When you manifest your desires and life purpose consciously, you care about how the Universe and the Law of Attraction respond to you, and you spend time and energy deliberately adjusting your vibrational frequency to manifest specific desires into your life.

On the other hand, when you're an unconscious manifestor, you manifest your desires by default. You let your vibrational frequency be influenced by external people and circumstances, and so what comes into your life depends on what you're exposed to.

Working your light involves empowering yourself with conscious manifestation techniques and processes that you can use to bring your life purpose, and the specific desires aligned to it, into your life. Having nurtured your light, you then have a raw resource of light to mould into whatever you want.

## Three Steps to Conscious Manifestation

According to spiritual teachers Abraham-Hicks, there are three main steps to the manifestation process:

1. **You Ask for What You Want:** The first step involves consciously or unconsciously asking for an improved state of being, or a specific desire.

2. **The Universe Manifests Your Desire in Vibrational Form:** As soon as you have a desire, the Universe instantly manifests that desire for you in a vibrational way. It also launches a process of gathering the various components that'll manifest that desire into your life in physical form.

3. **You Receive the Physical Manifestation by Getting in Vibrational Alignment with Your Desire:** All the desires you've ever desired are stored in your very own vibrational safe (what Abraham refers to as the *Vortex*), ready for you to receive in physical form. To open the door to your safe and let the desires flow into your life, you need to align yourself with their vibrational frequency.

From this perspective, conscious manifestation is all about the third step. Step one occurs whether you want it or not, step two is not your job and step three is all you need to focus on to manifest your life purpose, or anything else you want for that matter.

## Unlocking Your Vibrational Safe

To open your vibrational safe and let your desires and life purpose unfold physically into your life, you need to be in vibrational alignment with your desires and purpose. What does that really mean, though?

If the Universe responds to your vibrational frequency, and therefore your emotions, then you need to match your emotions to the vibrational frequency where you already have that which you desire.

For example, if you desire going on a cruise around the Mediterranean, you need to raise your vibrational frequency to the degree that it matches the vibrational frequency of being on that cruise. In other words, you need to feel how it'd feel like if you were on the cruise.

## The Key to Your Vibrational Safe

What would it feel like if you already had a specific desire in your life? How would it feel if you were already following and fulfilling your life purpose? Although the emotions you come up with will vary slightly, they'll all have one thing in common: they'll be positive, happy emotions.

You could say, then, that the vibrational frequency of having anything you desire is the vibrational frequency of the emotion of happiness *as it relates to your specific desire* (more on this in the next chapter).

Think about it; what would you feel being on that cruise? Happiness. What would you feel driving a new car? Happiness. What would you feel after getting a promotion at work? Happiness. What would you feel while following and thriving in your life purpose? Happiness.

As a rule of thumb, you can say that the key to opening your vibrational safe and letting all your manifested desires into your life is mastering and embodying the emotion of happiness. When you get happy, you're in alignment with your light and inner being, and as a result, everything in your life begins to flow more easily.

## Your Dominant Emotional State

That being said, it's important to note that the Universe responds to your dominant emotional state rather than your fleeting moment-to-moment feelings. Therefore, it is only when you establish a consistent feeling-place of happiness that you're able to truly master conscious manifestation and let your desires manifest in your life.

The good news is that you've now spent a considerable amount of time so far in this book nurturing your light and developing a happiness practice. The door to your vibrational safe has already begun to open, and it'll keep doing so the more time you dedicate to nurturing your light. The aim of this part of the book is to teach you processes that amplify your connectedness to your light and leverage it in a conscious way for manifestation, and in relation to specific desires.

139

# Chapter 24

# THE EMOTIONAL SIGNATURE

In the previous chapter, I shared that the key to opening your vibrational safe is to consistently embody the emotion of happiness as it relates to a specific desire. I call this desire-specific emotion of happiness the emotional signature of a desire.

Although this unique emotional signature is at the vibrational frequency of the emotion of happiness, it doesn't need to be the emotion of happiness as such. Instead, the emotional signature of a desire could be any positive emotion at or near the vibrational frequency of happiness. Such an emotion could be the emotion of love, joy, freedom, fun, enthusiasm, ease, balance, etc.

To come up with the emotional signature of a specific desire, simply ask yourself how it would feel if you had this desire in your life. Then, reach for the emotion or emotions that come up. Keep milking these emotions until you've saturated your body with them, and you've pinpointed a single emotion that best captures the vibrational frequency of having your chosen desire.

For example, the emotional signature of being in a fulfilling romantic relationship isn't necessarily the general emotion of happiness, but the way a happy, fulfilling relationship feels. To me, the emotional signature of a fulfilling relationship is the emotion of ease. It is still a happy emotion, but it's way more specific than that, matching the way I perceive my chosen desire.

## The Emotional Signature of Your Purpose

There are two ways you can go about consciously manifesting your life purpose:

1. **Embody the emotional signature of your life purpose.** Revisit your Life Purpose Declaration in Chapter 6 and go through the process of identifying its emotional signature.

2. **Embody the emotional signature of desires relating to your life purpose.** Break down your life purpose into smaller projects or desires, and then find their unique emotional signatures. For example, if your life purpose involves being a spiritual teacher, smaller desires aligned to it would be writing and publishing a book, creating an online course or speaking on stage.

My suggestion is that you choose the former approach and work on consciously manifesting your life purpose as a whole. This will let the Universe decide on the specific desires you should go after and the order in which you should do so, rather than you micromanaging every step of the way.

Whichever approach you choose, make a note of the emotional signatures that you come up with and keep them handy to use in the following chapters' processes.

# Chapter 25

# MAGNET OF ATTRACTION

Magnet of Attraction is my most powerful manifestation process, and the one I've used on a daily basis for years to manifest my desires and life purpose. It involves identifying the emotional signature of a desire and embodying it consistently, so that your entire body and being emanate the vibrational frequency of it.

I first came up with the process while at university, where I'd spend many hours every day becoming a magnet of attraction for various desires. It always worked wonders for me, and I know that it'll do the same for you.

The reason this is my go-to manifestation process is because it demonstrates how the Law of Attraction works almost instantly. By choosing and focussing on a specific emotion for a few minutes, you immediately start attracting specific words, thoughts and ideas related to it. As you do this each day, the emotion you focus on gains momentum and progressively attracts inspired ideas, action steps, opportunities, divinely coordinated circumstances and eventually physical manifestations.

Another benefit of this process is that it focusses exclusively on emotions rather than thoughts, which is more aligned with how the Law of Attraction works. As a result, by practicing the Magnet of Attraction process, you train yourself to feel rather than think your desires into manifestation. You'll find that this is a much easier and direct way to manifest than going the old-school way of micromanaging your thoughts.

## How to Become a Magnet of Attraction

Follow these steps to become a magnet of attraction, relating to either a single desire or your life purpose as a whole:

1. Identify the emotional signature of your desire using the guidelines in Chapter 24, and then define it as a single emotion.

2. Take a piece of paper, or use a whiteboard, and write the emotion in the centre.

3. Ask yourself repeatedly, what does this emotion feel like? Close your eyes and try to feel the emotion, while simultaneously searching for other similar-feeling emotions. Draw lines out and around the word, jotting down the emotions you come up with. This is the same process you used to come up with the emotional signature of your desire, but in this process, you go deeper with the aim of increasing the momentum of the emotional signature.

4. At some point, as you start embodying your chosen emotion, you'll naturally be inspired to jot down specific words, thoughts or ideas related to that

emotion. Write them down, too. This is the Law of Attraction working instantly to expand your emotion into increasingly more specific outcomes.

5. Continue the process until you've filled the entire page.

As you practice this process consistently, and as the emotional signature of your desire gathers momentum, you'll be inspired to take specific action relating to your chosen desire, and the Universe will bring opportunities and physical manifestations relating to it, too.

Just recently, I practiced this process using the emotion of effortlessness. I longed for more ease and flow in my life, so I set out to embody this emotion daily for thirty days. Just two weeks into the process, I started witnessing the results as manifestations started pouring into my life. I was invited to record a studio song for *Wonderland The Musical*, called Go With The Flow (notice how directly aligned the title is to my chosen emotion), I was asked to be a book mentor (something I've been wanting to do for a while) for the publisher That Guy's House (the publisher of this book) and I experienced an inflow of spiritual mentoring clients.

Now it's your turn! Practice the Magnet of Attraction process for at least thirty days and see what comes up. Then, send me a direct message on Instagram (@georgelizos) and share your manifestations with me.

# Chapter 26

# VISUALISATION DONE RIGHT

Manifestation visualisation is the conscious act of imagining yourself already living a specific desired outcome. When done right, visualisation can amplify your dominant emotional state and give the Universe extra details as to what having that desire in your life looks like. The more you effectively visualise, the stronger your dominant emotional state becomes and the faster you're able to manifest something in your life.

Due to its ability to add detail and stronger momentum to the manifestation process, visualisation is one of the most powerful tools for conscious manifestation. However, most people can't get it to work. Not because they visualise wrongly or not as strongly, but because they don't get the timing right.

## Getting the Timing Right

The degree to which visualisation works depends on the degree to which your dominant emotional state of being can support the specificity of what you're visualising.

Let's say you've just come out of a long-term relationship and feel devastated. If, from the emotion of devastation you visualise being in a fulfilling romantic relationship with the aim of manifesting a new one, you'll feel like you're mocking yourself. You'll be amplifying your negative emotion rather than dissipating it. From this perspective, visualisation works against you.

If you don't first take the time to heal, nurture your light and cultivate the emotional signature of the ideal relationship, visualisation, and any other manifestation process you use, will be pointless. Since the Universe responds to your emotions, all manifestation processes should be practiced *after* you've already nurtured your light and the specific emotional signature of your desire.

When you visualise yourself living this ideal relationship, after you've taken the time to heal and nurture the emotional signature of an ideal relationship, the specifics of what you visualise will amplify the already positive emotion you're feeling. Therefore, you'd be feeling that emotional signature even more potently, speeding up the Universe's response to your emotional offering.

## Visualisation Process

Use the following process to practice visualisation in an effective way that amplifies your dominant emotional state, allowing you to manifest specific desires with more ease:

1.   Choose a specific desire you'd like to manifest, or your life purpose as a whole.

2. Use the guidance in Chapter 24 to identify the emotional signature of this desire.

3. Spend at least five to ten minutes embodying the emotional signature of your desire. Be sure you're feeling this emotion fully before you move onto the next step.

4. Having embodied the emotional signature of your desire, begin visualising yourself already living its manifestation. Use all of your senses to do that, gradually adding more details. Be mindful of how adding details to your visualisation feels; be as specific as your emotional state of being allows. If at any point you feel negative emotion, it means you've gone too specific, too soon. Take a step back by visualising in a more general way.

5. Stay in visualisation for as long as you want, provided that it feels good. As a rule of thumb, ten to fifteen minutes of visualisation daily is enough to amplify your manifestation efforts.

6. When you feel complete, come out of visualisation and go on with your day.

# Chapter 27

# MAKING AFFIRMATIONS WORK

Positive affirmations were a catalyst for my spiritual growth. I first discovered the practice of using affirmations for manifestation during my bachelor's degree in Metaphysical Sciences. Soon after, I was introduced to Louise Hay's teachings on affirmations, and that's when life really started shifting for me.

I loved the idea of reprogramming my subconscious mind with new thoughts and beliefs that supported the person I wanted to become, and so I committed to doing affirmations on a daily basis. Having read all of Louise's books, and obsessed over her audio recordings, I filled my room with post-its of my favourite affirmations.

Everywhere you looked you could read:

*All is well in my world.*

*I'm open and receptive to abundance from expected and unexpected sources.*

*Life loves me.*

*I'm willing to change and grow.*

*Things are always working out for me.*

My obsession with affirmations lasted for at least five years, during which time I memorised entire affirmation scripts (I can almost recite Louise's *101 Power Thoughts* audio in its entirety from memory), and the results were astounding! By repeating and embodying the affirmations, I eventually managed to let go of beliefs that didn't serve me and fully committed to the new, positive beliefs I was affirming.

Of course, this process wasn't linear. My ego would come up and try to sabotage the whole process, and so I had to do a lot of inner work to identify and release past hurts and resentment that were tied to my negative beliefs before the new ones could come in and take their place. It was a long process of untangling and rebuilding my entire belief system about life, but it was totally worth it.

## A New Way of Using Affirmations

As a result of my obsession with affirmations, I perfected a way of using them effectively to not only change my beliefs, but to also use them as a powerful tool for manifestation.

At their very core, affirmations are conscious statements that you make about yourself, other people and the world at large. In my opinion, affirmations aren't negative or positive, they simply are. The degree to which they work in a positive or negative way for your manifestation efforts depends on the emotional state you maintain in relation to a specific desire.

For example, in the case of feeling disheartened following a breakup, the affirmation, 'I'm in the process of healing my heart,' isn't objectively positive, but it's more positive than the feeling of being disheartened. Therefore, in the emotional state of feeling disheartened, this affirmation works effectively in manifesting a fulfilling relationship.

## A Formula for Effective Affirmations

When you approach affirmations from a relative perspective, it becomes clear that an effective affirmation needs to satisfy two conditions: it has to be both positive and believable.

It has to be positive in relation to your current emotional state towards a desire, but not too positive that it feels impossible, or else it will worsen your emotional state. The affirmation needs to help you move up the emotional scale. It should act as a step towards improving your current emotional state.

It also has to be believable, otherwise it will work against you. You need to be able to feel, in your current emotional state, that while it may be a stretch, it's possible for your chosen affirmation to become a reality.

The ultimate aim of affirmations is to progressively move up the emotional scale until you can consistently vibrate at the emotional signature of your desire.

## Using Affirmations to Manifest Your Life Purpose

To put this affirmation formula into practice, let's consider your chosen desire, whether that is your life purpose as a whole or a specific desire related to it.

What are your current inner thoughts, beliefs or your emotional state regarding the manifestation of this specific desire? If your desire is to get a publishing deal, your current thoughts about it could be:

*I don't write well enough to be a published author.*

*I don't have a big enough platform to be picked up by a publisher.*

*I need to have lived life before I'm ready to write a book.*

*My ideas aren't good enough to be published.*

Alternatively, what would a positive, believable affirmation be in regard to these limiting thoughts?

You *could* go for, 'I'm a New York Times Bestselling author,' but although this is positive, it's not really believable in your current emotional state, and neither is, 'I have a huge audience that raves about my work!'

On the other hand, you could go with something like, 'I'm in the process of becoming a better writer,' or 'I love the people I'm already serving, and I'm constantly attracting more of them to my community.'

Do you see how the latter two affirmations were both positive and believable in the context of an existing negative thought pattern?

## Do the Work

How would this process play out in terms of your specific desires? Take some time to brainstorm new affirmations in your journal, and once you've come up with a few of them, and after you've confirmed that they feel both positive and believable, get in the habit of doing the affirmations daily.

You can include them in your morning and evening rituals, or you can follow my example and stick them on post-its somewhere you can see them at least a few times during the day. When you come across them, pause, take a deep breath, say the affirmations out loud and allow yourself to feel and embody them.

If you want to take this process a step further, go through all your specific desires concerning your life purpose, or anything else you desire, and create affirmations for them. Post these all around your room or house, and let them saturate your consciousness.

As mentioned earlier, the aim of affirmations is to progressively move up the emotional scale until you can eventually feel the emotional signature of your desire in a consistent way. Therefore, it's important to always feel good while doing your affirmations. When you no longer feel that way, it means that you've moved up the emotional scale and it's now time for you to create new ones.

# Chapter 28

# MANIFESTATION ALTARS

An altar is a bridge between the sacred and the secular; between heaven and earth. It's a physical creation that acts as a portal for Source Energy to enter the physical realm, allowing us to have an easier, deeper interaction with it. Although Source flows through everything and everyone, and connecting to it should be effortless, creating altars is a way for us to satisfy our ego's need for portraying Source in a physical way, while focussing our intention and facilitating mindfulness.

All indigenous traditions and cultures of the world have used altars in their spiritual practices. Since the beginning of time, humans have felt a need to build physical altars as a way of inviting Source into their daily lives, routines and religious and spiritual practices.

From a manifestation standpoint, altars serve two purposes:

Firstly, setting up an altar shifts our perception of manifestation from 'getting the Universe to work for me' to 'collaborating with the Universe to manifest my desires.' As discussed in earlier chapters, for many years we've been taught that manifestation is getting the Universe to do our bidding, which is a disempowering way of thinking about manifestation. An empowering reframing of this belief is that manifestation is really divine collaboration. Altars help us to access the energy of the Universe in a more palpable way, facilitating this kind of co-creation.

Secondly, altars have the advantage of giving form to the formless. They allow us to express the emotional signature of our desires in a physical way, so that we may better embody it. When crafted effectively, manifestation altars generate the vibrational frequency of our desires and keep it active for us 24/7, working on our behalf to bring the physical elements of our desires into our lives.

## Space and Memory

As part of my bachelor's degree in Geography thesis, I studied the relationship between physical space and memory. Specifically, I set out to answer the question: *Is memory constructed in a physical space or does space absorb people's thoughts, emotions and memories, storing them within its ethers?*

I concluded that both theories are, in effect, correct. We can manufacture memories within a physical space by changing the design with colours, buildings, sounds and symbolism. Think about how you feel when you walk into a Zara clothing store versus how you feel when you walk into a Hollister store. Zara's interior design is clean and simple, while Hollister's is rich with colours, scents, music and video. Don't you think and feel different in each one of them? Walking into Hollister makes me feel like I'm a surfer in LA, whereas stepping into Zara feels more urban.

At the same time, memory is also stored in the ethers of a physical space. Whatever you think, feel and experience within your house is stored in vibrational form in the energy of the house. Have you ever noticed how your behaviour sometimes changes after you've moved into a new house? It almost feels like you've become a different person. This happens because the energy of the house's previous inhabitants, along with what they experienced while living there, still lingers in the ethers of the physical space, influencing you in a subconscious way.

## Creating Your Manifestation Altar

Creating a manifestation altar, then, is a way for you to consciously construct the emotional signature of a specific desire within your home or another physical space, so that you instil that space with the energy of your desire. Doing so tunes the energy of your home to the energy of your desire, which in turn influences your own personal energy.

That being said, it's always a good idea to clear the energy of your house before you build your manifestation altars, so as to bring it to a neutral state. This will make it easier for the constructed energy of your manifestation altar to saturate your space. You can space clear your house yourself by researching space-clearing processes, or you can ask a professional space clearer to do this for you.

Creating a manifestation altar involves bringing together various deities, objects, symbols, colours, crystals, mudras, invocations and essential oils that best capture the emotional signature of your desire, with the intention of getting them to work for you in attracting that desire in your life.

Follow these steps to create your manifestation altar:

1. Choose your desire and identify its emotional signature using the guidelines in Chapter 24.

2. Choose a small space or corner within your house in which to create your altar. It can be something as simple as a corner of your desk, a side table, somewhere on the floor or even a bookcase shelf.

3. Your altar should ideally include the following elements:

   a. A figurine or image of a spirit guardian to look after your manifestation.

   b. Candles to activate the energy.

   c. One or more of the five elements of earth, air, fire, water and spirit, to add to your desire's energy.

   d. Crystals that relate to your desire.

   e. Colours that best capture your desire's essence.

   f. Various symbols and items that further add to its essence.

   g. An essential oil that you feel holds the energy you want to bring into the manifestation process.

4. Putting your altar items together is more an art than a science. The idea is to group together these elements in a visually appealing way, which will help ignite within you the emotional signature of your chosen desire.

5. Before you've finalised your altar, ask yourself, *How does this make me feel?* The aim is that your altar holds the essence of your desire's emotional signature. If it doesn't feel that way, keep moulding it and re-arranging the items until you hit the mark.

By setting up your altar, you've already started the process of collaborating with the Universe in order to manifest your desire. Your altar acts as a portal of communication between you and the Universe, or whichever deity you choose to work with, and the symbolism of the altar instils in you and your space the emotional signature of your desire, speeding up the manifestation process.

In the next chapter, you'll learn a simple ritual for activating and further enhancing your altar's effectiveness, so that you can manifest your desire faster.

# Chapter 29

# MANIFESTATION RITUALS

Whereas creating a manifestation altar helps instil the emotional signature of your desire into your house, which then affects your own personal energy, a manifestation ritual is an act that you perform at your altar with the aim of directly embodying the emotional signature of the desire within you.

Manifestation rituals are powerful amplifiers of emotion. They help you to embody the emotional signature of your desire in a powerful and lasting way, making it easier for you to reach for the frequency of your desire in your day-to-day life, thereby speeding up the manifestation process.

A manifestation ritual essentially involves focussing your intention on your chosen desire while inviting the Universe to respond to it in a much stronger way than you normally do. It's the perfect formula for divine collaboration.

Before you're ready to use your altar for a manifestation ritual, you first need to consecrate and activate it.

## Consecrate Your Altar

Consecrating your altar means purifying the energy of both the space that the altar is set-up in and the items you've chosen to build it with. Physical space will, along with the items you've collected, absorb vibration from their surrounding environment, plus the energy of people that have interacted with them. Consecrating your altar and altar items resets their energy, so that they can better receive (and align with) the emotional signature of your desire.

Follow these steps to consecrate your altar:

1. Choose one of the many tools to consecrate your altar, such as burning incense, using sound, sprinkling water or simply sending your inner light channelled through your hands.

2. Bring your chosen tool close to your heart. With eyes closed (and where applicable), call upon the spirit of the tool to activate its power and support you in this process.

3. Use the tool to clear your altar in an intentional, ceremonial way. For example, if you're using lit sage, wave the smoke above, below and around your altar with the intention of it purifying all, or activate your hands with your own inner light and send love to your altar.

4. When you feel that the space has been cleared and purified, place the tool close to your heart and thank it for its assistance.

## Activate Your Altar

After you've consecrated your altar, activate it with your intention, i.e. dedicate this sacred space to helping you embody the emotional frequency of your desire, so that you can manifest it.

Follow these steps to activate your altar:

1. Place your hands in prayer position and focus your attention on the centre of your heart. Visualise a bright, golden light extending from your heart to your palms. This light is pure Source Energy.

2. Extend your hands outwards to face the altar, visualising the light washing over all the altarpieces and the surrounding space, instilling it with loving energy and intention. Stay here for as long as it takes for your altar to feel elevated.

3. Dedicate the altar to your chosen desire by setting your intention either mentally or out loud. You can say, 'I dedicate this altar to the manifestation of [state your desire]. Thank you for helping me embody and amplify the emotional signature of my desire, so it can manifest in my life at the perfect time.'

4. When you're done, place your hands in prayer position to close the process.

## Perform a Manifestation Ritual

Rituals have been used around the world since time immemorial. As a result, there are infinite ways to perform a manifestation ritual. There are simple rituals and there are elaborate rituals. There are rituals timed to coincide with specific cosmic events and occurrences, such as the phases of the moon, the solstices and equinoxes, and there are rituals involving all sorts of religious or spiritual beliefs, incantations and connotations.

The way I've used ritual to manifest my desires has varied over the years. Growing up Christian, I'd light up beeswax candles and use Byzantine icons of various saints to pray for the manifestation of a specific desire. When I transitioned to New Age, I called upon various deities and angels, and used symbols, mantras, music and colours to create long and elaborate rituals. I even went through a Wicca phase, utilising manifestation spells to help to work my magick.

These days, having transitioned to Greek paganism, I work with various Greek deities, recite Orphic Hymns and provide offerings and libations as part of my manifestation rituals.

The best thing about trying different rituals from different belief systems is that I know for sure that they all work. The reason they do is because the single element that ensures a manifestation ritual works has nothing to do with certain religious beliefs. Instead, it's got everything to do with belief, intention and how the Law of Attraction truly works.

## What you Focus on Will Grow

When you focus your attention on something while embodying its emotional signature, the Universe has to respond with an equal physical manifestation equivalent. The bells and whistles that you choose to include in your rituals – e.g. sayings, mantras, prayer, hymns, precessions, offerings, libations, etc. – only serve the purpose of helping *you* focus your intention while embodying the emotional signature of your chosen desire.

Thus, the role of your religion or spirituality is to help you get in touch with your inner power, so that you believe you can manifest whatever it is you desire, and focus your attention in a way that helps you bring that desire into your life.

Rather than giving you instructions on the way that I perform manifestation rituals, I'll instead provide general guidelines that you can apply to your own belief systems, so that you can create a manifestation ritual that works for you.

## Ritual Procession

Follow the following guidelines to plan and create your manifestation ritual:

1. **Call Upon Your Guides:** The ritual starts by calling upon the Guide(s) you've chosen to help manifest your specific desire. This is the Guide you've

included in your altar. It could be an angel, the Universe, a pagan god/goddess, Jesus, Mother Mary, a Saint, an Ascended Master or anyone else you want to bring in. Start by mentally or verbally inviting the Guide to support you in this process. You could say, 'I call upon Apollo to guide this ritual. I ask you to guide me in performing this ritual in the best possible way for me to embody the emotional signature of [state your desire] to its fullest, so that I may manifest it in my life at the right time, when I'm ready.'

2. **Light Up the Candle:** With intention, light up the candle on your altar, symbolising both the beginning of the ritual and the enduring support of your Guide in the manifestation process.

3. **Embody the Emotional Signature of Your Desire:** The middle part of the ritual involves using various methods of embodying the emotional signature of your desire. This is where your spirituality will come in. You can recite mantras, set an intention, read a hymn, burn your fears in pieces of paper, write down your desire in great detail, pray, sing a devotional song or programme a crystal. Do whatever it is that makes sense for you, to help you feel – *truly* feel – what your desire would feel like if it were already manifested in your life.

4. **Offer Gratitude:** The final step in a manifestation ritual involves offering gratitude to your chosen Guide, as well as to yourself, for guiding you

through the ritual. You can also ask your Guide to stay with you for as long as it takes for the desire to manifest in your life, consciously working to keep its emotional signature active within you. At the end of the ritual, make sure to let the candle burn completely. If you use a bigger candle, let it burn for at least three hours. This is more than enough time to activate the energy within the altar and yourself.

## Extending Your Manifestation Ritual

Your manifestation ritual needn't be finished at the end of the ceremony. You can easily sustain the energy that you've nurtured during your ritual in the days, weeks and months that follow, until your desire has manifested. I like to keep the manifestation altar active for at least 30 days after I perform a ritual. This is usually enough time for the desire to manifest in my life, or for me to embody its emotional signature to the degree that I no longer need the altar or the ritual to help me do so.

After your ritual, print out a 30-day calendar and commit to performing a daily mini-ritual at your altar. This needn't be long; you can simply call upon your Guide(s), light up a candle, do a short prayer and offer gratitude. You can let the candle burn for at least three hours, knowing that for the duration that it's burning, the initial ritual is still actively working for the manifestation of your desire.

I like to include this mini-ritual in my morning spiritual practice. It helps me to start my day right by embodying the emotional signature of my chosen desire while reaffirming my trust in the Universe and my guides, all of which contributes towards manifesting the desire in my life.

# Chapter 30

# HOW TO RECEIVE CLEAR SIGNS FROM YOUR GUIDES

Visualisation, affirmations, Magnet of Attraction, manifestation altars and rituals are my preferred, and the most powerful, processes for working your light. When done right, they will get you into a state of being where you can receive signs and divine guidance from the Universe, your angels and your spirit guides regarding the specific action steps you need to take in order to bring your desires and life purpose into manifestation.

That being said, what usually prevents many lightworkers from moving forward with their purpose, and thus from working their light, is their inability to perceive the signs and divine guidance that come after the practice of conscious manifestation.

What's more, despite the overwhelming number of books, courses and processes out there on psychic development, many of us still find it hard to know for certain if the inklings we have come from Source or from our own ego.

Rather than reiterating the plethora of psychic development information that's already out there, in this chapter I'll instead offer my top four processes and hacks to help you fine-tune your intuitive ability to receive clear signs from your guides.

To learn more about psychic development, check out my online workshop with fellow psychic Carrie Stiers *Psychic Hit* at GeorgeLizos.com/Shop

## Ask for a Small Sign First

We've all seen the movies, read the books and heard the stories where angels show up to save the day when it seems like all is lost, clouds form in the shape of Jesus to reassure those in need or a departed grandma whispers to her granddaughter that she's on the right path. Our world and the media glorify miracles and other profound revelations of spirit to such a degree that they inevitably direct our expectations of what a true sign from spirit is or should look like.

As a result, we have rigid expectations as to the specificity of and medium through which divine signs are given, which prevents us from acknowledging the subtler and more common ways through which spirit communicates with us.

The grand signs usually come to people whose disbelief in the spirit world is such that they need something grand and unequivocal in order to believe in divine guidance. They ask big, so the Universe's response has to be equal in size. If you already believe in the existence of the spirit world, your angels and guides take for granted your ability to receive their signs, and they'll in turn send you subtler, but no less poignant, signs to follow.

To break free of the expectation for signs to come in specific ways, sizes and mediums, it helps if you ask for a small and specific sign first. Doing so retrains you to expect simple, almost mundane signs, rather than the glorious divine revelations you're programmed to expect. This also ensures that your ego doesn't doubt the validity of the sign when it shows up, as it's not something completely out of the ordinary.

Examples of small and specific signs you can ask for are feathers, a specific-coloured car, word, song, animal or any other object that's meaningful to you. Simply close your eyes and ask for the Universe, your angels or spirit guides to send you this specific sign with the single purpose of showing their presence. You can do this while you're reading this right now, and then see what comes up over the next few hours.

## Decide on a Communication System

Another reason many lightworkers have difficulty receiving divine guidance is because they haven't specified the communication system through which they want their guides to communicate with them. Although your guides and the Universe have every intention of communicating with you, they're constrained by the fact that they're non-physical. Their language is different to yours, and so to communicate effectively, you have to meet them halfway.

The easiest way to do this is to tell your guides which communication system you want them to use when they send you signs. Psychic communication systems can include popular divination systems, such as tarot and oracle card decks, runes, numbers or a meaningful category of everyday items, such as colours, songs, flowers, etc. The difference between a single sign and a communication system is that the latter is a group of signs from the same category, which allows for the transmitting of more detailed divine guidance.

The way I communicated with my guides when I was first starting out on this path was through card decks and numbers. I'd predefined the meanings of certain numbers, so that my guides knew what number or combination of numbers to send me to communicate specific messages. If I needed to delve deeper, I'd use a tarot or oracle card deck that allowed for more specific detail.

## Find Your Intuition Language

Your intuition language or languages are the primary senses through which you receive intuitive messages. In the same way that we perceive physical images, sounds, feelings, tastes and smells through our sensory system, we perceive intuitive messages, too.

Traditionally, these intuition languages are known as the six Clairs:

Clairvoyance, meaning clear seeing.

Clairaudience, meaning clear hearing.

Clairsentience, meaning clear feeling.

Clairgugstance, meaning clear tasting.

Clairalience, meaning clear smelling.

Claircognisance, meaning clear knowing.

Although we all receive intuitive messages through all six Clairs, we all have one or two that are predominant. I'm naturally claircognisant and clairvoyant, meaning I receive divine guidance as a clear and unequivocal knowing of something, or through visions and visual signs, both physical and intuitive.

Knowing the primary channels through which you receive guidance from your spirit guides curbs your self-doubt and focusses your attention on expecting signs and guidance through these channels.

## Finding Your Dominant Clairs

Although you generally come to find your dominant Clairs through experience, the following questions will help you gain more clarity:

1. Close your eyes and remember your last birthday party. How did you spend it? Where were you, and what did you do? Who was there, and what went on? Replay the entire event in your mind.

2. What's your fondest childhood memory? Allow yourself to go back and remember it fully.

3. What was your biggest accomplishment? Go back in time to remember the moment you achieved it. How did you feel? Who did you tell? How did things unfold?

Take some time to either replay these three occurrences in your mind, or perhaps journal about them. These were all moments in your life where your sensory system was particularly stimulated. Through which sense did you most experience these events? Did you mostly see, feel, hear, tasted, smelled or know things? Which one or two senses were most active?

## Is it Ego or Intuition?

Probably the biggest block that lightworkers have to overcome in order to receive clear, intuitive guidance from their guides is understanding whether the guidance they receive comes from ego or Source. Although we explored the main differences of ego and intuitive guidance in Chapter 21, the following three indicators will help you to understand this further:

1. **If it's intuition, you've already followed it.** Intuitive guidance is so unequivocal that you don't spend time doubting or considering it. You take instant action towards it because your whole being screams that it's true. If you doubt, second-guess or have to ask other people's opinion, it most probably isn't intuitive but ego guidance.

2. **Intuitive guidance comes instantly.** You can tell the difference between ego and intuitive guidance by observing the timing in which the guidance shows up. Intuitive guidance is the first to come, followed by ego guidance shortly after. Almost always, ego

guidance will try to doubt or sabotage intuitive guidance, whereas intuitive guidance is pure and positive.

3. **Intuitive guidance feels expansive.** It feels light and uplifting, whereas ego guidance feels contractive and heavy. You feel these emotions in your body. In any moment of receiving guidance, you can tune into your body to sense how it feels. Is there tension (ego) or relief from tension (intuition)?

Each time you catch yourself wondering if the guidance you're receiving comes from your ego or your intuition, go through these three indicators to get clarity. If you end up getting confused, take a break from the whole thing and ask for a clear sign from your guides. It's always easier to get new guidance rather than analyse old guidance. Your guides will happily send an avalanche of signs your way until you get it.

Use the guidance in this chapter to train yourself in receiving clear signs and communication from your spirit guides and Universe, on the way to following your life purpose. As you commit to your manifestation processes, the signs will show up, and they'll be the perfect steps for you to take to move forward with your chosen desires and purpose.

## Chapter 31

# UNICORN MEDITATION: YOUR NEXT STEPS TO FOLLOWING YOUR PURPOSE

Having developed your manifestation toolkit and gotten clarity on how to receive guidance from the Universe and your guides, all that's left to do is to do the work. Choose the manifestation processes that work best for you and commit to them, being mindful of the guidance that comes forth as a result.

If you do the work but the guidance isn't coming through, then chances are that you're not allowing it to come through, or you're just not seeing it. This is when you can lean on your Unicorn Guide for support.

Remember, your Unicorn Guide is an extension of your soul. It's inherently tied to your purpose, and it knows the exact pathway you need to follow to fulfil it. Do the following meditation when you get stuck, or if you need that extra confirmation that the guidance you're receiving is valid.

The more you work with your Unicorn Guide via meditation journeys, the more you'll awaken your intuition languages, strengthening your capacity to receive guidance.

## Unicorn Meditation for Your Next Action Steps

1. Close your eyes, breathe deeply, relax your body and come into a meditative state.

2. With your mind's eye, visualise a tiny dot of golden light in the centre of your heart. Your heart is the doorway to your soul, and the golden light lets it in.

3. With every inhale, visualise the golden light growing outwards until it fills up your chest and body, and extends outwards to envelop your aura. Bask in the energy of your soul for a few minutes.

4. Mentally call upon your Unicorn Guide to make itself present.

5. As your unicorn shows up in your awareness, it presents you with a large digital screen, similar to the ones you see in movies. As the screen turns on, it showcases a future projection of yourself already taking the necessary steps to reach the next level of your purpose. You may see, hear, feel, taste, smell or know what's shown on the screen – use your intuition language to perceive what's being presented to you, and don't feel like the process is not working if you can't visually see things clearly.

6. Ask your Unicorn Guide for more details and clarifications on the steps you're meant to take. What are your fears or frustrations regarding these steps? What needs to change before you can follow them?

175

7. Finally, your Unicorn Guide points its horn, the alicorn, towards you, and showers you with high-vibrational rainbow light: the Rainbow Ray. This light clears your chakras and aura and raises your vibration, equipping you with the state of being that you need to be in to take action.

8. As you come out of the meditation, thank your Unicorn Guide and ask it to stay with you and support you as you move forward.

9. When you're ready, take deep breaths, make small movements with your hands, head and shoulders, and then open your eyes and come out of the meditation.

You can download an expanded audio recording of this meditation at GeorgeLizos.com/LGW

## Chapter 32

# WHEN IN DOUBT, GET ON YOUR KNEES

Conscious manifestation is fun when it's all working out the way you expect it to. In a world that glorifies action taking and hard work, it feels good to visualise, affirm and then do the work to bring your desires into manifestation. However, what happens when your action taking doesn't yield the results you expected?

When conscious manifestation doesn't go as expected, most people go one of two ways:

1. **They lose trust in the Law of Attraction.** Rather than changing or adjusting their belief system to problem-solve and better understand how manifestation works, they lose trust and revert back to their default beliefs in struggle and hard work.

2. **They work their manifestation processes harder.** Although their belief in the Law of Attraction stays intact, they believe that they haven't worked hard or well enough to make the processes work. As a result, they obsess over the mechanics of the processes and put in more effort.

Which of the two approaches have you taken when your manifestation efforts didn't work out the way that you expected them to?

## The Real Purpose of Conscious Manifestation

The reason why many people have a hard time using processes to consciously manifest their desires is because they don't truly understand the purpose of conscious manifestation.

Although it is true that what you give out must come back to you, the timing of when it'll come is unknown to you, but perfectly known to the Universe. The purpose of conscious manifestation isn't to control the timing of when something shows up, but simply to place your order with the Universe and trust that it'll come. It is then up to the Universe to consider your order and come up with the perfect time-space sequence for its delivery.

Consider going for dinner at a restaurant. Do you expect the food to show up immediately after you've ordered? Do you call on the waiter every five minutes, protesting that your food isn't there yet? Do you storm into the kitchen and scream at the chef for not preparing it faster?

In a restaurant, you understand that a good meal takes time to prepare. You trust that the chef and his staff have made preparations long before you got there, to ensure that your meal comes to you in the perfect time-space sequence. You trust the process because you understand that food takes time to prepare, and that if you try to hurry the process, your meal won't be as tasty.

The manifestation of your desires works the same way. When you take action by using manifestation processes, you place your order with the Universe. It'll take some time for the Universe to prepare and deliver your order, but it'll come at the perfect time and when you're ready for it. However, if you keep doubting the Universe's ability, and constantly protest that your desires aren't there yet, you're only delaying the manifestation process.

## The Most Powerful Manifestation Process

The most powerful manifestation process is using no processes at all. This is the biggest paradox to manifestation, but once you get it, you'll master the game.

There's a difference between *needing* and *wanting* something. Needing implies that you don't have it yet, whereas wanting relays that although you don't need a specific desire to be happy, it'd be a nice addition to your life. When you need a desire, you feel the absence of it, but when you want it, you're indifferent whether it comes or not because you're happy without it anyway.

A common pitfall when using manifestation processes is the ease through which can shift from wanting to needing something. Remember the restaurant analogy? When you *need* your order instantly, you doubt its delivery, but when you want it, you trust that it'll come when it's ready.

There are many ways to shift from needing to wanting while practicing manifestation processes, but because the distinction is very subtle, sometimes it's just easier to cease practicing all processes. Letting go of all manifestation processes and just trusting that the Universe will deliver your desires at the perfect time works equally well, if not better than using conscious manifestation processes.

From this perspective, why bother with manifestation processes in the first place? When done right, using manifestation processes will ease the way through which a desire shows up in your life. As you focus your intention and energy more intently, you *help* the Universe prepare and deliver your order, and thus you become a more active co-creative component in the manifestation process. When done right, conscious manifestation results in your having fun and enjoying the journey every step of the way.

The best approach, then, is finding the right balance between conscious manifestation and completely surrendering to the Universe. The key to achieving this is paying attention to the way you feel while consciously manifesting something. When you use your emotions as your guidance system, you can easily tell when you've shifted from wanting to needing.

Wanting feels good, while needing feels bad. When using manifestation processes stops feeling fun and exciting, it means you've shifted to needing, and vice versa. As soon as something no longer feels fun for you, it's the time to abandon the manifestation process and either reach for another one or surrender completely.

## How to Surrender

Surrendering is a popular concept in manifestation, yet many teachers use it in an abstract way. In other words, what does surrendering truly mean? What do we surrender and how do we do it?

Many people falsely believe that surrendering implies letting go of the desire altogether. In truth, surrendering is about letting go of the need or resistance that we hold, which blocks the desire from manifesting. When we surrender our resistance, we allow the purity of our desire to resurface within us, without the doubt and impatience that blocks manifestation.

Having pondered the concept of surrendering over many years, and practiced several processes, I've ended up with three practical and effective steps you can use to surrender your resistance and allow the manifestation process to take place:

## 1. *Get on Your Knees*

Your body is your ego's most emblematic tool; it's what differentiates you from other people and the rest of the world. Your body represents your sense of independence, which as we learned in an earlier chapter, is only *part* of who you are. In truth, you're connected with all that is, and are one with everyone and everything. Therefore, when you get on your knees out of a desire to surrender your resistance, doubt, frustration or any other negative emotion that's blocking the manifestation process, you surrender the power of your ego. You subconsciously and symbolically tell your ego that it's powerless in the face of Source. You simultaneously remind the ego that it's not the one running the show and invite your inner guide to take over.

You can get on your knees to surrender anywhere you feel comfortable. You'll find it's probably more effective when you're practicing this in private, or a sacred place such as your altar, a temple, church, out in nature or anywhere else that's sacred to you. There are no specific rules as to how to surrender this way, other than requiring a willingness to let go and let Source take over.

## 2. Open Your Arms to the Sky

This is a powerful mudra to use when you need to surrender, which has the added benefit of opening you up to receiving guidance as to how you can move forward with your manifestation efforts.

When praying and honouring the gods and goddesses, the ancient Greeks held their arms open to the sky as a way of opening themselves up to the wisdom and guidance of the gods. When you practice this power pose, your heart chakra, which is the doorway to your soul, opens up so that you can feel more clearly your soul's wisdom.

## 3. Declare Your Willingness to Be Guided Out Loud

Thoughts have more power when uttered out loud. There's something about expressing ourselves in a verbal way that gives our thoughts more power. Declaring your willingness to surrender and be guided out loud makes it more real. Your willingness stops being an illusory thought in your mind and gains more substance.

As a result, because you feel your words more fully, you're more likely to surrender your resistance and trust that the Universe has your back. I usually express my desire to surrender by combining all three processes. I get on my knees at my altar, open my arms to the sky and declare out loud:

*'I let go of the need to control the manifestation of this desire. I surrender to the wisdom of the Universe, and trust that this desire will come to me at the perfect time and when I'm ready. I know that only good comes to me at all times. Universe, thank you for taking my resistance and taking control of this situation.'*

The more palpable you make your desire to surrender, the more powerful the surrendering will be, as will the subsequent guidance that flows through. Not because Source isn't listening, but because we perceive Source listening more when we express something in a more physical way.

There are countless ways to surrender; these are simply three processes that I've found work exceptionally well in releasing resistance and opening me up to the wisdom of the Universe. Try these processes at least once and see how they work for you. Feel free to adjust them, change them or discard them completely and go for something that helps *you* find the feeling of surrender.

Create your own surrendering process if you must, and use it every time your manifestation efforts stop feeling fun and exciting. If you focus on the way something feels, and only do things that feel good, you can't get this wrong.

# PART IV

# PROTECT YOUR LIGHT

Chapter 33

# WHY PROTECT YOURSELF?

It was 30 December 2016, and I was in Cyprus for the holidays when I got a call from a popular national TV channel. They invited me to go live on their morning show the following day for a 30-minute segment, to give people guidance on setting their intentions for the New Year.

To say I was excited about it would be an understatement. This would be my first TV appearance, and a great opportunity to get exposure. The interview would be in Greek, which despite being my first language, is not the language that I feel most comfortable speaking. It was clear that I'd need to do a great deal of prep for it, and I barely had enough time to get it done.

I dedicated the entire evening and following morning to preparing for the interview, and I was so caught up in the excitement and preparation for it that I forgot to shield myself before going live. Long story short, the interview went great. I performed at my best, the audience loved it and so did the presenters.

However, as soon as I got off the set, it hit me... Suddenly, I was overwhelmed by strong feelings of nausea, dizziness and a piercing pain in my stomach. I drove home and went straight to bed, and I stayed there for the following two weeks.

I realised what went on as soon as it had happened, but by then it was too late to do anything about it. I was psychically attacked. I'd exposed myself to thousands of people sending all sorts of thoughts and energy in my direction, and had no shield with which to repel or filter them. As a result, I was like an energetic sponge, absorbing other people's energy until it burned me out.

I knew that psychic protection was important, but after that experience I realised that it wasn't just important, it was necessary.

## What is Psychic Attack?

Traditionally, the term psychic attack refers to someone consciously or unconsciously sending an intense wave of negative emotion, usually anger or jealousy, your way. However, I've chosen to expand the definition of psychic attack to encompass a wider variety of ways through which we can be affected by negative energy. Although the most severe cases of psychic attack do come from people, I feel it's important to have a broader understanding of how external energy can negatively impact us, so that we can better protect ourselves.

Just like physical attack, psychic attack hurts physically, emotionally and mentally. The effects of it can last for as long as an hour to months, depending on the intensity of the attack.

Here are the most common symptoms of psychic attack:

- Fatigue, Exhaustion
- Headaches
- Feeling cold
- Unexpected physical pain
- Nightmares
- Dizziness
- Feeling like you can't breathe
- Unexpected depression
- Mood swings

There are many levels and types of psychic attack. Some are obvious and intentional, and therefore easily recognizable. Others are more subtle, working in subversive ways to drain our energy and leave us feeling depleted.

The most common types of psychic attack are:

- Psychic daggers of jealousy and anger
- Low-level spirits feeding off of your energy
- Collective thought forms and energy
- Residual spatial energy that you pick up through the day

- Toxic cords of attachment to people, things, places and past lives

## Why Protect Your Energy?

While reading my psychic attack story, you might have caught yourself wondering, *What about TV presenters, actors, and singers? Do they all psychically shield themselves before going on stage? If not, do they all get psychically attacked?*

Although some of them do shield themselves in one way or another, most of them probably don't. As discussed earlier, psychic attack manifests to varying degrees and in different ways for different people, so even though not everyone experiences the same effects that I did, they do become affected in other ways.

That being said, lightworkers are far more susceptible to psychic attack than other people because we're more sensitive to energy. As such, it's easier for us to feel for, and subsequently be receptive to, other people's energy, as well as energy in our environment. In many ways, this is a gift, since it allows us to connect to people on a much deeper level. However, if unmonitored, this gift can easily become a burden.

Additionally, because we naturally see the good in people, we often share too much with those who may not have our best interest at heart, both verbally and energetically. As a result, we expose ourselves to more judgement, jealousy, and attack than the average person.

189

Lastly, our world has become increasingly interconnected, meaning that we interact with more people daily than we used to, both in real life and on our social media platforms. Simultaneously, more and more people are becoming aware of their psychic abilities and the potential of using energy in a conscious way. Although most spiritual seekers use their intuitive skills as a force for good, some don't. As a result, being fiercely protective of our light and energy is more important now than ever before.

## Is Protection Feeding Fear?

Sometimes, when I express to people my reasoning behind protecting our energy, they respond by saying that doing so gives power to fear, thus making us vulnerable to attack.

The truth is that I'm in complete agreement with this statement, but I still think protection is important.

In spiritual truth, there cannot be any form of attack, whether psychic or physical. We're all one source of consciousness, and therefore we cannot attack our own self. When we see life from our inner being's perspective, and know and feel our love and connectedness, we cannot be attacked by anything or anyone. The most powerful psychic protection tool, then, is not believing in attack or the need to protect ourselves in the first place.

That being said, could you confidently say that you see life from the perspective of your inner being 24/7? Unless you spend most of your time meditating, you probably don't. If we were meant to be constantly purely connected to our inner being, we wouldn't have been born into this physical world. We came here with an ego and a sense of separation, not to reject it, but to use and co-create with it.

I personally take for granted that, although there will be moments in my day where I'll feel 100% aligned with my inner being, I'll be disconnected from it to various degrees for the majority of the day. There's nothing wrong with that; it's just part of being human.

From this perspective, it would be equally as naïve to not protect my energy as it would be to not take precautions when I'm out and about, or while browsing online. Don't you tend to avoid walking down a dark street by yourself at night? Aren't you extra careful with your personal possessions while traveling? Don't you protect your online identity by setting up strong passwords and avoiding opening scam emails? If so, why would you treat your energy in a different way?

The aim of this last part of the book isn't to scare you or to make you vulnerable to psychic attack; it's meant to empower you with knowledge and processes that you can use to protect your energy *when you need to*. My advice is that you do your best to maintain your alignment to your inner being, which is your most powerful protection tool, and use these methods when you're out of alignment or need an extra boost.

# Chapter 34

# TYPES OF PSYCHIC ATTACK

In the previous chapter, I introduced the five most common types of psychic attack. To better understand how to protect yourself from them, it's important to understand the mechanics through which each of them works.

## How Psychic Attack Works

### *Your Aura*

You're not just your physical body. You have many different other bodies that exist within and around your physical presence, but in parallel dimensions. This is commonly known as your aura, or auric field, which extends up to 4ft outside of your physical body.

An aura can be defined as the life force energy of both animate and inanimate objects, and its structure depends on the complexity of each object. For example, a human aura is more complex than the aura of a fork or knife.

The human aura has seven main layers corresponding to the seven chakras, each one extending outwards from the centre of your physical body into the surrounding environment. These are the etheric, emotional, mental, astral, etheric template, celestial and causal bodies, and they all have different functions and properties. Each layer, or body, of your auric field exists within the other, while extending progressively further than the one which precedes it.

Due to their fluid and volatile nature, auras can flow between objects, both sending and receiving energy. It is your aura that allows you to sense the energies of people and places as you walk through life, constantly giving you feedback about the world around you. Due to its heightened perceptive abilities, if unprotected, your aura acts like a sponge that absorbs all kinds of energies from people and places. Unless consciously cleared, this energy remains stuck in your aura and affects the way you think, feel and exist in the world.

## Your Chakras

Your chakras are energy portals found in specific locations in the centre of your body, where they act as mediums of communication between your physical and spiritual sides. You have seven main chakras, each one governing a set of physical, emotional, mental and spiritual aspects of yourself. These are the root, sacral, solar plexus, heart, throat, third eye and crown chakras. You can learn more about the specific qualities of your chakras in my previous book, *Be the Guru*.

Since the seven layers of your aura are extensions of your seven chakras, any psychic attack picked up by your aura feeds through to the core of your chakras. Concurrently, as bridges between your physical presence and the spiritual, energetic world around you, your chakras also have sponge-like qualities and tend to absorb energy from other people and your surrounding environment.

Although your seven chakras have unique characteristics and energies, and are found in distinct locations within your body, they're also interconnected. There's an energetic channel flowing in a zigzag pattern through all, so psychic attack on one chakra may affect the entire system.

## Five Types of Psychic Attack

Let's go over the five main types of psychic attack and how they can manifest in your reality:

### 1. Psychic Daggers of Jealousy or Anger

Often referred to as the evil eye, these are manifestations of other people's jealousy of, or anger towards, you, and what is traditionally referred to as psychic attack. Since we live in an energetic, vibrational world, whatever we think and feel also has energy. When we direct this energy at another person, we send a wave of toxic energy towards them. If unprotected, the other person receives this energy unconsciously, in the form of an energetic imprint on their aura or chakras, blocking their flow of energy.

If you're clairvoyant, you'll probably see these imprints manifesting as etheric daggers, knives and other types of conventional weapons on your back. You may also perceive them as dark masses of energy, cobwebs or stains. These psychic daggers may also be perceived as feelings and sensations, similar to the examples given in the previous chapter.

## 2. Collective Thought Forms

This is the subtlest, and therefore most unexplored, type of psychic attack. When a large group of people think or feel at a certain low vibrational frequency long enough, they give that energy life and beingness. The traumatic events of 9/11 in New York City, for example, created a huge mass of fearful energy that lingered in the atmosphere long after what had happened (and to some extent, it's still there now). That energy stayed in the ethers of the city subconsciously, affecting people as they went about their daily affairs.

Don't different cities and countries feel different to you? This is partly because of the collective thought forms that exist within each place, being thought and felt into being by the inhabitants.

Collective thought forms tend to be more severe in large megacities, where there's a great deal of people going through similar negative circumstances, or in places where there are high levels of crime and terrorist attacks. If you've lived in big cities such as London, Hong Kong and New York, and also in smaller cities and rural villages, you'll have certainly felt their contrasting energies. The fears and frustrations that come up within you, simply by virtue of being and living in a big city, are far more intense than the ones that come up in smaller towns and villages.

## 3. Low-Level Spirits

I believe that there's no source of evil, but instead the absence of love. When love is absent, the negativity and disconnection that ensues can give form to all sorts of being-less spirits and energies, creating what I refer to as low-level spirits. In truth, these spirits only exist because someone thought them into existence. They survive by feeding off of other people's fearful emotions, which are in resonance to that low vibrational frequency.

As a rule of thumb, at different vibrational frequencies you have access to different spirits and energies. You can only attract negative spirits and entities, including all other forms of psychic attack, when your vibrational frequency is lower than the vibration of your inner being.

When you're going through a hard time and are feeling down emotionally, or when you're intoxicated by drugs, alcohol or other substances, your vibrational frequency lowers. In this state, you're more susceptible to attracting, and therefore feeding, low-level spirits and energies that match this vibrational frequency.

## 4. Residual Spatial Energy

This is a minor type of psychic attack that involves picking up energy that's been left lingering in the ethers of physical space by other people, hence why it's referred to as 'residual.' Since both animate and inanimate objects have an aura, and auras both send and receive energy, the physical spaces we live in – our homes, neighbourhoods and cities – can be thought of as oceans of the auras of all the people and objects that exist within them. As we move through physical space, we litter the energy of the space with our energetic imprints. Whether this is positive or negative energy depends on our current emotional and mental state.

Residual spatial energy is different from collective thought forms in the sense that it hasn't gained enough momentum yet to grow into its own being and affect a large group of people. Instead, this subtle energy is scattered in physical space, and we unconsciously pick it up while going about our daily affairs. Common symptoms of this milder type of psychic attack include feelings of fatigue, exhaustion, brain fog and headaches.

## 5. Toxic Cords of Attachment

These are attachments that you have to people, places, things, beliefs or past lives, as well as attachments that others have to you. Our humanity demands that we have attachments to things, with psychologists distinguishing between secure and insecure attachments. Secure attachments are positive attachments that we have to our friends, family, things and places we love, in which we're not needy of or dependent upon them for happiness.

Insecure attachments, on the other hand, are rooted in co-dependency. It's when we feel like we need someone's attention to feel complete, or that we need a substance, thing, belief or being at a certain place to feel happy and at ease. Sometimes, other people have insecure attachments to us, and both directions of attachment can be considered forms of psychic attack, because in both cases, we're the ones on the receiving end of the negative feeling that the insecure attachment is creating.

Many teachers don't usually consider toxic cords of attachment as a type of psychic attack, because sometimes we're the ones choosing to create the toxic attachment. I personally see these cords as the most powerful type of psychic attack, *because* we're the ones choosing the attachment. Since from a state of oneness and alignment with our inner being there isn't such a thing as psychic attack, it's not really us who choose to create a toxic attachment to someone or something, but our ego. Toxic cords of attachment, then, can be thought of as self-psychic attack.

This type of psychic attack is the toughest one to deal with and protect from, because it's not something that we simply pick up on a daily basis. Instead, these negative cords are rooted in the time and energy we've invested in nurturing relationships with people, places, objects, beliefs and past lives. As a result, these cords are constantly feeding off of our energy, draining and leaving us feeling lifeless and depleted.

Now that you're aware of the main ways through which you can get psychically attacked, we'll spend the following chapters exploring powerful ways of protecting your light and energy.

# Chapter 35

# HOW PSYCHIC PROTECTION WORKS

In the following chapters, you're going to learn a number of techniques to clear and shield your energy, as well as to manage your energetic attachments. However, beware that when you fill your spiritual toolkit with all of these protective bells and whistles, it's easy to become dependent on them. This defeats the whole purpose of using them.

The most empowering realisation I've had while learning and experimenting with different psychic tools and processes over the years is that the most powerful tools in our possession, and the only tools really, are our own body and intention.

We come into the planet equipped with a natural, inherent programming that allows us to connect to and work with energy. Every single cell in our bodies is intelligent and works as a portal of communication with the divine. Giving our power away to physical tools and psychic processes limits what we can allow ourselves to receive and experience.

All psychic protection tools and processes do is help to amplify our own natural abilities for protection. So, while reading through and applying the psychic clearing and shielding techniques in the following chapters, be mindful of the attachments that you create to these techniques, and always remind yourself that *you* are the one that truly holds the power to protect your energy.

## The Power of Intention

As I mentioned in Chapter 33, when you hold a strong belief that there's no such thing as psychic attack, you can't be affected by it. This belief projects a powerful intention that you are always protected and aligned to Source, and your intention automatically casts all the protection 'spells,' clearing and shielding you, and keeping you aligned to your inner being.

Similarly, when using the psychic protection tools in subsequent chapters, it is your intention to use these tools that casts protective layers over your energy, not the actual processes themselves. If you take your focussed intention out of the equation, you rid the process of its power and effectiveness.

When you set out to try these processes, always take some time to close your eyes and feel your power. Ground into your body and see yourself aligned to Source; know your power and focus on your intention of clearing or protecting your energy. Then, and only then, will you be able to start using the suggested processes effectively.

## The Law of Free Will

In a few of the clearing and shielding processes, you'll be asked to call upon spiritual beings. Again, it can be tempting to give your power away to these guides that seem external to, and more powerful than, yourself.

Firstly, it's important to remember that these beings aren't separate from you in the same way that you're not separate from anyone or anything in the entire Universe. In spiritual truth, we're all one, and that includes angels, elementals, spirit guides and Ascended Masters. When you connect to these guides, you're simply connecting to an extended part of your own being.

Secondly, these guides cannot help you if you don't give them permission to. Therefore, it also requires an intention to receive help. The Law of Free Will says that spiritual beings can only help you if you give them permission to. Yes, in spiritual truth you're connected and One with them, but in this incarnation, you manifested as a separate physical being because you wanted the free will to do as you wished.

In the processes where you have to call upon these spirit guides, ensure that you mentally set your intention and give your permission for them to help, while knowing that by doing so you're really receiving help from a higher, extended part of yourself. Doing this will ensure that you don't become dependent on these beings for support and protection, but that you instead call upon them if and when you need to.

## Setting Clear Intentions

Although I'm sure that by now you understand the importance and power that your intention has in clearing and protecting your energy, you may be wondering exactly how you can express your intention in an effective way.

In the processes that I'll guide you through in the following chapters, you may wish to express your intention in one or more of the following ways:

- **Visualisation:** This is focussed and conscious imagination. During processes, you'll be asked to visualise light, etheric cords or spiritual beings. The very act of conjuring up an image in your mind establishes your intention to work with these beings throughout all processes.

- **Thoughts:** If you're not a visual person, you may choose to mentally think about or will these processes into effect. Rather than visualising light surrounding you, you may simply mentally think it into being. Your thoughts are equally intent-laden as your visualisations.

- **Words of Affirmation:** The third way you can use intent to bring these processes into effect is to simply state what you want to experience out loud. You can make up a simple affirmation, such as, *'I shield myself with protective rainbow light, intending that it stays with me for the duration of the day and protects me from all negative energy and people.'*

- **Written Words:** The final way of expressing your clear intention for clearing and protection would be to write things down in your journal, on a document on your computer or on a piece of paper. The act of writing something down makes it real. Sometimes, when we spend too much time in our minds, our focussed intentions get lost in our usual mind chatter. When we express our intentions in written form, we separate them from the rest of our thoughts, giving them more power.

If it helps you focus, you can use any combination of these four ways. You can visualise yourself surrounded by light while thinking, writing and verbally affirming its protective qualities.

# Chapter 36

# SCANNING FOR PSYCHIC ATTACK

Before you attempt any clearing or shielding processes, it's important to first know what you're dealing with. Scanning for psychic attack involves using your primary intuition languages to identify the five types of psychic attack that we discussed earlier within your energy field.

If you've never cleared your energy before, you'll most likely encounter a great deal of psychic attack that needs to be released. Don't let this alarm or scare you in any way, as you'll learn how to expertly release all of it in the following chapters.

Scanning and clearing yourself for the first time will likely take a great deal of time and energy, but as soon as you're done, you'll be able to complete the entire process in no more than ten minutes each day. I personally scan, clear and shield myself as part of my spiritual practice every morning. It's become a daily habit, as essential as brushing my teeth and putting my clothes on. Ever since I started doing this, I've noticed palpable shifts in my energy, wellbeing and manifestation abilities.

## Turn on Your 360-Degree Vision

Before you're ready to scan yourself for psychic attack, you have to turn your intuition on. There are many ways to do so, but my preferred way involves a technique that my spirit guides taught me early on in my spiritual journey. It involves turning on my 360-degree vision.

Although your human body is restricted to perceiving the world around you via your physical eyes, your spiritual bodies are multidimensional and have the ability to perceive all directions at once. This technique allows you to shift your attention from your physical to your spiritual dimensions, which awakens your intuition and allows you to perceive psychic attack in a much more palpable way.

Here's how you can turn on your 360-degree vision:

1. While in meditation, focus on your third eye chakra, which is found in the centre of your head, in between your eyebrows. Your third eye chakra is the control centre of your intuition, allowing you to shift your vision from the physical to the spiritual planes. Visualise your third eye chakra as a bright ball of purple light that grows bigger with each in-breath. Breathe deeply until your third eye chakra grows so big that you feel a shift in your energy.

2. Now that your third eye chakra is activated, you can start awakening your 360-degree vision. Without opening your eyes, visualise what's right in front of you. Use your mind's eye to get a sense of

the energetic dimension of the physical world facing you. Don't overthink this or second-guess yourself. Simply observe what's coming up.

3. While maintaining your inner vision of what you're seeing in front of you, expand your vision to 'see' what's on your right and left, so that you see it all at once.

4. Expand your vision further, so that you can see what's above and below you, while at the same time seeing what's in front of you, to your right and left.

5. Finally, expand your vision even further, so that you observe what's behind you while still seeing the world in front of you, to your right, left, above and below. Stay in this awakened state for a few minutes, allowing your body to adjust to your newfound 360-degree vision.

## Psychic Scanning Process

Having awakened your psychic vision, you're now ready to scan your body for psychic attack. Ideally, use the following scanning process as soon as you've finished turning on your 360-degree vision:

1. With your 360-degree vision activated, turn your attention to your physical body, so that you can observe its energetic dimension and the first layer of your aura, known as the etheric body. Scan

through your body and look for any discordance; you may find psychic daggers, collective thought forms or residual spatial energy appearing in the form of dark energy, vibrational stains and etheric cobwebs. Remember, depending on your primary intuition language, you may not visually see these, but rather perceive them via a difference sense.

2. Now, look closer within your etheric body to identify toxic cords of attachment extending out towards other people, objects, places, beliefs and past lives. Many of these cords tend to be attached to your chakras, specifically your heart and solar plexus. Are these cords that *you* have created or that others have attached to you? You can get a sense of this by mentally 'touching' the cords and paying attention to the way you feel. This will help you get a sense of the relationship and understand the nature of the attachment.

3. Move your attention away from the toxic cords and focus exclusively on your seven chakras. What do they look like? Are they clean and vibrant, or murky and dim? How would you describe their health? Are there any psychic daggers piercing through them, or dark energies clouding them? What types of psychic attack can you see there, if any?

4. Finally, expand your awareness to observe the layers of your aura that extend all around you. Here, you may see collective thought forms manifested as dark stains of energy, low-level spirits, residual spatial

energy or other bad vibes that your aura has absorbed over time. Simply observe these without judgement.

5. When you've finished scanning for and identifying psychic attack within your body and aura, come out of meditation. Make a note of what you've identified in your journal, so that you can clear it later, or move straight into the processes in the following chapters.

Chapter 37

# PSYCHIC CLEARING TECHNIQUES

Before you shield yourself to protect from psychic attack, it's important to first clear your energy, otherwise you'll simply be shielding the psychic attack in. If you've never cleared your energy before, or you only seldom do so, then chances are that you've accumulated a great deal of psychic attack in your subtle bodies. This negative energy affects the way you think, feel and act in the world, and unless you clear it, you're essentially allowing other people's energy to control you.

In this chapter, you'll learn ways to clear psychic daggers, collective thought forms, residual spatial energy and low-level entities. You'll learn how to deal with cords of attachment in the following chapter.

## Nature is the Most Powerful Protector

There are many methods you can use to psychically clear your energy of psychic attack. You can use crystals, essential oils, flower essences, incense, bells and singing bowls; you can work with angels and Archangels, your spirit guides and other Ascended Masters. The list is endless.

My preferred way of clearing my energy involves partnering up with the elementals, as I believe that all the answers we seek are found in nature. Since ancient times, people have channelled the earth's wisdom to heal their mind, body and spirit, and the world's cultures are rampant with teachings of the powerful healing qualities of nature.

The earth has innate processes that she uses to clear out toxic energy and maintain her balance. Her various processes, including those in the atmosphere, ocean currents, plate tectonics, rivers and volcanoes, all work together to both destroy and create energy, ensuring that our planet keeps on thriving no matter what.

Rather than reinventing the wheel and making up our own clearing processes, we can simply tune into the earth's already proven and established ways, and channel them on a personal level. Doing so involves connecting with the nature spirits, the elementals of earth, air, water, fire and spirit, as introduced in Chapter 16.

Having worked with the elementals for over ten years, they've taught me practical processes that I use to both clear and shield my energy. In this chapter, I will introduce three of these processes that focus on clearing your etheric body (the first layer of your aura, which exists within the constraints and is the energy side of your physical body), your aura as a whole and your chakras.

## Clearing Your Etheric Body with Dragon's Breath

When I refer to your etheric body, I refer specifically to the energetic dimension of your physical body, the first layer of your aura. Your etheric body is an extension of your root chakra, and therefore controls your physical health and energy levels and your relationship with the physical world around you, as well as your drive and motivation in life on the way to following your purpose.

Psychic attack within your etheric body manifests primarily in the form of psychic daggers, collective thought forms and residual spatial energy that you pick up on a daily basis. These types of psychic attack tend to affect you on both a physical and an emotional level, as you experience them in the form of physical illness, fatigue and lethargy, as well as a strong sense of anxiety, worry and fear around issues of survival.

The fire element and the collective energy of the fire dragons are best equipped to help you clear the energy of your physical body, due to their ability to transmute energy. In this process, you'll call upon the transformational qualities of fire through the fire dragons, to both clear unwanted energy from your etheric body and recalibrate it with pure-positive life-force energy.

Here are the steps to the process:

1. Closing your eyes, come into a meditative state. As you take long, deep breaths, notice the warmth of

your body. The essence and energy of fire flows through you, and allows you to connect easily with its guardians, the fire dragons.

2. Expand your awareness to see how the element of fire manifests around you and in nature. Notice how fire manifests in the electric appliances you use, in candles, bonfires and in the warmth of the sun. Mentally observe fire burning in the core of the earth, in the magma below its surface and the lava erupting in volcanoes all around the world.

3. Having connected with the collective oversoul of fire within and around you, mentally or out loud call upon the collective energy of the fire dragons to make themselves present. You could say, *'I call upon the collective oversoul of fire and the fire dragons to flow through me and clear my etheric body from all that no longer serves me.'*

4. As you say this, you may notice the presence of fire dragons flying above your head, or even the presence of your dragon guardian from the element of fire coiling around your body. Take some time to make your acquaintance with the dragons and thank them in advance for the clearing.

5. Ask the dragons to blow their divine fire trough your body, with the aim of burning all psychic daggers and other toxic energy that's blocking the natural flow of vitality. Simultaneously, the fire will also revitalise your physical body, leaving you

feeling energised and uplifted. Breathe deeply as this process takes place, and notice as the psychic daggers and other negative energy in your body disappear.

6. After the process has finished, take some time to offer gratitude to the dragons, thanking them for their service.

7. Once you feel ready, come out of the meditation and drink some water to ground yourself, allowing your body's energy to adjust to the changes.

You can download an expanded audio recording of this meditation at GeorgeLizos.com/LGW

## Clearing Your Aura With a Sylph Storm

As I mentioned earlier, your aura is made up of seven layers that are extensions of your seven main chakras, extending up to 4ft in all directions around your body. To a clairvoyant, it looks to be an egg-like cocoon of light enveloping your physical body. Each layer of your aura corresponds to different areas of your life and wellbeing. Whereas the first layer of your aura tends to attract psychic daggers, the other six layers attract mostly low-level spirits, collective thought forms and residual spatial energy.

The sylphs, the collective elementals of the element of air, are powerful guides that help us to clear and recalibrate our auras. Doesn't the energy of your house always shift when you open a window and let fresh air in, and don't you always feel uplifted and energised while outside on a particularly windy day? The constantly moving, ever-changing qualities of the wind can move energy like no other element, and the sylphs are the spirits that drive this.

It's the sylphs that orchestrate tornadoes and hurricanes year after year, and although these are catastrophic for humanity, they're necessary repercussions of the environmental destructions we create, and the earth welcomes them with gladness.

In this process, you'll call upon the oversoul and collective essence of the sylphs to energetically clear your aura from any unwanted energy that clogs it.

Here are the steps to the process:

1. Closing your eyes, come into a meditative state. As you take long, deep breaths, notice how the element of air manifests in your body. Observe as your chest expands and shrinks with each breath, as it welcomes the vital oxygen in the air. Notice how much more peaceful you are as you become mindful of your breathing.

2. Expand your awareness to notice how the element of air manifests in the world around you. If you're outside, feel the gentle caress of the wind on your face and see it gently rustling through the plants, flowers and trees all around you. Become aware of

215

how the atmosphere fills up the entire planet, acting as the connecting link between all planetary consciousnesses.

3. As you connect to the collective essence of air, mentally or out loud call upon the collective energy of the air sylphs to make themselves present. You could say, *'I call upon the oversoul of air and the air sylphs to flow through me and clear my aura from all that no longer serves me.'*

4. As you say this, you may notice the presence of slender, almost formless air sylphs flying playfully above your head and around your body, or even the presence of your sylph guardian from the element of air. Take some time to make your acquaintance with the sylphs and thank them in advance for the clearing.

5. Ask the sylphs to start circling through and around the periphery of your aura in a clockwise manner, clearing your aura of negative energy. They progressively fly faster and faster around you, picking up momentum and creating a powerful windstorm or tornado that removes low-level spirits, thought forms and all other negative energies from your aura. Breathe deeply during this process, allowing the sylphs to work their magic.

6. After the process has finished, take some time to offer gratitude to the sylphs, thanking them for their service.

7. Once you feel ready come out of the meditation and drink some water to ground yourself, allowing your body's energy to adjust to the changes.

You can download an expanded audio recording of this meditation at GeorgeLizos.com/LGW

## Clearing Your Chakras with Fairy Dusting

The types of psychic attack that you can expect to find clogging your chakras are primarily psychic daggers, collective thought forms and toxic cords of attachment (we'll deal with the cords in the following chapter). However, what tends to clog your chakras more than external psychic attack is internal psychic attack. Your chakras are extensions of you, and they mirror the way that you think, feel, act and perceive yourself and your world as you go through life. Therefore, the state of your chakras depends more on your inner state of being, as it relates to the various qualities and life areas that each chakra governs.

The elementals most equipped to help us clear our chakras are the elementals of earth, and specifically the flower fairies. Each flower has unique healing qualities, and working with essential oils and flower essences are powerful ways of partnering up with flowers to experience healing in mind, body and spirit. Working with the spirits within various flowers is also very effective, especially when dealing with the delicate energy of our chakras.

Although you can partner up with the flower fairies of specific flowers to clear different chakras, calling upon the collective energy of flower fairies works equally well. Your body knows which flower(s) it needs on a spiritual level, and it'll call on the right blend of flower fairies to bring upon healing.

Here are the steps to the process:

1. Closing your eyes, come into a meditative state. As you take long, deep breaths, notice how the element of earth manifests in your body. Become aware of your body's texture, its weight and the way it is present in the space you're in.

2. Expand your awareness to notice how the element of earth manifests in the world around you. Notice the earth beneath you, along with the plants, trees and flowers that inhabit it. Beyond that, observe the element of earth in all physical life around you, including both animate and inanimate objects. Realise that all physicality is an extension of the earth element.

3. Mentally or out loud, call upon the collective energy of the flower fairies, which are part of the earth elementals, to make themselves present. You could say, *'I call upon the oversoul of earth and the flower fairies to flow through me now and clear my chakras from all that no longer serves me.'*

4. As you say this, you may notice the presence of tiny fairies of light flying above your head, or even the presence of your flower fairy guardian(s) from the element of earth. They'll appear in any way that makes sense to you. Take some time to make your acquaintance with the fairies, and then thank them in advance for the clearing.

5. Ask the fairies to clear all your chakras, starting from your root and moving up all the way to your crown. As the fairies gather around each chakra, they'll send healing sparkling light, or fairy dust, to your chakras. This light expertly clears all blocks and rebalances the flow of energy through your chakras.

6. After the process has finished, take some time to offer gratitude to the fairies, thanking them for their service.

7. Once you feel ready, come out of the meditation and drink some water to ground yourself, allowing your body's energy to adjust to the changes.

You can download an expanded audio recording of this meditation at GeorgeLizos.com/LGW

These three elemental practices are perfect for clearing your energy of most forms of psychic attack. You may use them intermittently, perhaps if you feel like you've attracted some kind of attack, or you can use them regularly to ensure that you're constantly cleared of external negativity. I use all three processes every morning as part of my spiritual practice, and I'm surprised to see that, despite the daily clearing and shielding, I still have energies to release the following day.

As with all practices in this book, feel free to adjust them so that they work with your preferences and belief system, or use them in combination with other processes that work for you.

## The Energy Purge

If this is the first time you've cleared your energy of psychic attack, you may experience what's known in energy healing as an energy purge. When you release toxicity on an energetic level, you'll then also release it in an emotional, mental and physical way. Your various bodies and chakras are interconnected, so when you create a change in one of them, it also affects the others.

You may experience this purge as a short-term worsening of your emotional, mental or physical condition; you may notice your thinking becoming more negative as you experience mood swings, get short-tempered more often or get angry for no reason; or you may even experience flu-like symptoms and headaches. This is all normal. It's simply your body releasing what you've released energetically and adjusting to your newfound energy.

The purge usually lasts between a few days and a couple of weeks, after which you'll notice a profound improvement in your wellbeing.

Although you've now cleared most types of psychic attack from your energy, you still haven't dealt with toxic cords of attachment, which is what we'll cover in the following chapter.

## Chapter 38

# CUTTING TOXIC CORDS OF ATTACHMENT

Just like there are multiple ways that you can clear your etheric body, aura and chakras, there's also a plethora of tools, processes and spirit guides you can work with to cut toxic cords of attachment. However, my preferred way of cutting cords of attachment requires hardly any tools or spiritual beings, and instead involves purely the use of our physical bodies, specifically our hands.

As I mentioned early on in this part, your body and intention are the only tools that you really need to perform any kind of spiritual clearing and protection, and all other tools and spiritual beings are simply there to help amplify and support your own power. Although we could easily work with such tools and beings to cut cords of attachment, I find it's more effective to keep this a solely personal task, given the personal nature of these cords.

Unlike other types of psychic attack, such as collective thought forms, low-level spirits and residual spatial energy, which you often pick up spontaneously and unconsciously as you live life and interact with people and spaces, toxic cords of attachment are created deliberately over a long period of time. The majority of these cords are created as a result of the time and energy you consciously spend with people, such as the moments you share, the words you exchange and experiences you have together. While these cords might have been positive at the start of a relationship, they've eventually turned negative as the relationship has deteriorated.

The same is true of the toxic cords of attachment that you have to places, things, beliefs and past lives. Even though these aren't living beings, they still have an energy and beingness that you engage with. You have relationships with these places, limiting beliefs, objects and past lives in a similar way that you do with people.

I've found that due to the intimate nature of these relationships, fully releasing them requires an equally intimate process, and our own physicality is the perfect tool for it.

## Cord-Cutting Process

Follow these steps to cut and release the toxic cords of attachment you have to people, places, objects, beliefs and past lives that you've identified in your scanning session:

1. While getting into a meditative state, activate your 360-degree vision and bring back into your awareness the toxic cords of attachment extending out from your etheric body, and primarily your chakras.

2.  Spend some time observing each cord by gently touching and following it to see where it leads. As you engage with it, you'll get a sense of the person, place, object, belief or past life it is connected to. Be mindful of not stirring up anger, hurt or resentment during this process, as this only strengthens your attachment. Simply observe and make mental notes of what each cord signifies.

3.  Once you've identified all the cords, you're now ready to cut them and release these relationships. While sitting or standing up, with your eyes open or closed, come into your power to clear energy. Feel life-force energy flowing through you, connecting you to the heaven above and the earth below, and know and affirm that you have all it takes to completely release these toxic relationships.

4.  See your dominant hand (the one you write with) as a powerful tool to assist you in this process. When you are ready, extend your fingers so that your palm is wide and long, and swiftly run it through each cord, using your hand as an energetic knife to cut through them. While you do this, you may affirm, silently or out loud, *'I release you from my life fully and completely.'* Send love and gratitude to these people, places, objects, beliefs and past lives for all the lessons they've taught you. Avoid offering negative, angry or resentful energy, as this will prevent the cord from being cut. Take a couple of deep breaths between each cut to centre your energy.

5. Once you've cut all the cords, spend at least five minutes in quiet meditation to give your body time to adjust to the new changes, while continuing to send love and gratitude to what you've released.

6. When the process feels complete, come out of the meditation and take a shower to clear and ground your energy.

## Dealing With Sticky Cords

What's important to realise in regard to cutting cords of attachment is that the work isn't done when the cord is cut. When cutting the cord, you *energetically* release that person, place, object, belief or past life, setting the intention that you no longer wish to be negatively affected by them. That being said, your *physical* attachment to that being may still be in place. You may still see these people on a daily basis, entertain a negative belief or hang out in certain places, for example. As a result, often some of these cords may grow back, re-establishing your toxic attachments.

To prevent this from happening, you need to be willing to do the real-life work that will come up shortly after the cutting session. Having released these attachments energetically, and therefore changing your own personal energy, you'll attract situations, interactions and circumstances that will give you the opportunity to release these attachments in a physical way, too.

For example, you may get the chance to have a heart-to-heart conversation with some of these people, where you calmly but assertively end or transition your relationship with them. You may get an offer for a new job in a different city, or receive an impulse to make a change in your life that involves letting go of an object or substance that you've previously cut your cord of attachment to. You may be inspired to read a book, attend a workshop or take an online course that has exactly what you need to fully transcend a limiting belief or heal a past life trauma.

It's important that when these opportunities come up in your life, you take advantage of them. Your ego will surely come in and try to sabotage the healing process, appeasing these people, numbing your pain and keeping you in denial of what you've been through. This is the time to be mindful of such sabotaging thoughts, and have the courage to ignore them and take action towards completing the cord-cutting process.

We'll discuss practical ways of dealing with these sticky cords, particularly in regard to relationships, in Chapter 41.

# Chapter 39

# PSYCHIC SHIELDING TECHNIQUES

Now that you've cleared your energy of psychic attack, you're ready to shield it with protective vibrations and layers of light. Like all psychic protection processes, shielding works with your intention, and there are many different processes you can use to protect your energy from incoming psychic attack.

Similar to psychic clearing, my preferred way of doing so involves partnering up with the elemental beings and drawing from nature's toolkit. The two processes that I'm about to guide you through are the ones I use on a daily basis to protect my energy.

## Bathe in the Rainbow Ray

The Rainbow Ray, or simply Rainbow Light, is a very high-vibrational energy brought forth by high-dimensional, ascended beings of the element of spirit, such as the unicorns. Aside from your Unicorn Guide, who is a spiritual extension of your soul, you also have access to the collective essence of the unicorn realm, a part of the spirit element.

Consisting of all the colours of your chakras in their purest and highest-vibrating frequency of light, the Rainbow Ray has the ability to raise your vibration to such a height that you simply can't attract psychic attack. Psychic attack only affects you when your vibration is a match for it, which occurs when you're living from the perspective of your ego. When you raise your vibration by bathing in Rainbow Light, you're not a match for psychic attack or negativity in any form.

I first encountered the Rainbow Ray after connecting with my Unicorn Guide, Xeros, while teaching my online course *Unicorn Bootcamp*. Xeros, and the collective presence of the unicorn realm, guided me to let my unicorn's horn, the alicorn, touch each one of my chakras. They communicated that rather than being an actual horn, the alicorn was a high-vibrating light that had the ability to recalibrate every piece of consciousness that it came into contact with. At the touch of Xeros's alicorn on my chakras, I felt an explosion of energy surging through my body and instantly felt connected to Source.

What I didn't realise at the time was that this seemingly white light was actually the Rainbow Ray. It was only after cross-referencing this with my friend and author of *Unicorn Rising*, Calista, with whom I co-teach the *Elemental Healing™ Practitioner Course* that I could see this clearly. Aside from the fact that when you blend the seven colours of the rainbow together, they create white light, the colours within the Rainbow Ray are so high-vibrational that even when you perceive them singularly, their energy is so bright that all you can see is white light.

Since then, I've worked consciously with Xeros, the unicorns and the Rainbow Ray to bathe in this light daily. What I love about this process, particularly in comparison with the traditional white light bubble technique taught by most teachers, is that rather than having to *shield* myself, I instead bathe in this light. Although I use the term psychic shielding in this book due to its wide appeal, the very act of wanting to shield yourself from something negative gives power to, and attracts, the negative. By shifting your perception of these shielding processes in an empowering way, you add to their effectiveness.

Follow these steps to bathe in the Rainbow Ray:

1. Get into a meditative state and call upon your Unicorn Guide.

2. Once your unicorn makes its presence felt, spend some time observing its horn, the alicorn. Notice how blindingly bright it is, and realise its potency in recalibrating anything it comes into contact with.

3. Ask your unicorn to touch your third eye chakra with the tip of its horn. The Rainbow Ray will flow through from the horn into your third eye chakra, and then expand through your entire body and aura. As soon as this happens, you may feel a shift in your energy.

4. Let your unicorn transmit the Rainbow Ray for a few minutes, until you feel as though your vibration has risen to a significantly high degree. Once you feel you've received sufficient light, thank your unicorn and ask them to stop the transmission.

5. Spend some time meditating in this state. Visualise the rainbow light flowing through your body and aura, and ask it to stay with you for as long as you need today, so that you only attract experiences that match its high vibration.

6. When you feel ready, come out of the meditation and get on with your day feeling energised and uplifted.

You can download an expanded audio recording of this meditation at GeorgeLizos.com/LGW

## Wear the Violet Flame

The Violet Flame is a similarly high-vibrational energy. It's traditionally thought to be associated with Saint Germaine and Archangel Zadkiel, but when connecting to it I've always seen it carried by high-dimensional fire dragons. Depending on your perspective, you will receive this energy from a source that makes sense to you. This flame is different than the usual dragon fire that you've worked with to clear your etheric body, in that it operates at a much higher frequency to both clear and repel all forms of psychic attack and negativity. Although it may look similar to the violet colour of the Rainbow Ray, it is a completely different energy, which is why it's usually referred to as a flame rather than light.

Although the Violet Flame and the Rainbow Ray both have high vibrational frequencies, they express themselves in different ways, and therefore have different purposes. The Rainbow Ray uplifts and raises vibration, whereas the Violet Flame clears, transmutes and repels negative vibration. One activates, while the other dispels.

In this process, you will shield (or bathe) yourself with a layer of the Violet Flame to protect yourself against attracting psychic attack, and also to clear and transmute any attack that you've ended up attracting throughout your day. Due to the fact that the Violet Flame both clears and protects, it's a quick process to use daily for both psychic clearing and shielding.

Use the following steps to wear the Violet Flame:

1. Get into a meditative state and call upon the fire element and the Violet Flame Dragons. You could say something along the lines of, *'I call upon the spirit of fire and the Violet Flame Dragons to come into my presence and guide me through this process.'*

2. Rather than coming from the Violet Flame Dragons, the Violet Flame instead emerges from the ethers. It exists in the here and now, albeit in a different dimension. The dragons simply guide and direct the flow of the energy; all you have to do to

activate it within you is focus on and call upon it. When you're ready, say, *'I call upon the Violet Flame to come into my presence now. Thank you for flowing through my body and spirit, clearing and transmuting all negativity and protecting my energy for the duration of the day.'*

3. You will see the Violet Flame showing up through you and around you. At first, it'll look like normal violet light, but the longer you focus on it, the more you'll notice it burns and sparkles like fire. Visualise the Violet Flame enveloping your body and aura, clearing all negativity that still remains within your body. Rather than interfering with the Rainbow Ray, it works with it to make you invincible against external negativity.

4. Once you've established the boundaries of the Violet Flame shield within and around you, offer gratitude for its protection and come out of meditation.

You can download an expanded audio recording of this meditation at GeorgeLizos.com/LGW

## Psychic Shielding FAQs

As you experiment with these psychic shielding processes, along with other processes you might have learned along your path, you may find yourself asking questions in regard to their effectiveness, usefulness and frequency of practice. The following are the three most frequent questions that I get asked about psychic shielding:

## Are These Processes Foolproof?

Although all the processes I've introduced are powerful and effective in protecting you against psychic attack, they're not completely foolproof. They are as effective as your moment-to-moment vibrational frequency allows them to be. As you go through the various experiences of your day, your vibrational frequency drops and rises accordingly. Yes, the Rainbow Ray is there to keep it high, but you have the ability, through your focus on life's negative experiences, to diminish or enhance its potency.

Therefore, although the Rainbow Ray and Violet Flame will protect you from psychic attack to a great degree, you may still attract negativity as your vibration oscillates.

## How Often Should I Shield Myself?

Ideally, you should shield yourself every morning, setting the intention that the protection lasts for the duration of the day. However, given that your vibrational frequency will inevitably vary as you go through your day, it's safer to shield yourself a second time in the middle of your day, as a way of boosting your existing shields.

Simultaneously, you could strengthen or reactivate your Rainbow Ray and Violet Flame shields if at any point you feel exposed to external negativity, simply by intending it. I've often called upon the protective qualities of these energies while in a hospital, the gym, airport or whenever I'm exposed to a large group of people. When I do so, I immediately feel my shoulders relaxing and my mood lifting.

### Can I use these shielding processes in combination with others?

Yes, if you already have a psychic shielding practice that works, you don't need to change it. I would, however, suggest that you try these processes out at least once and see how they work for you. You may eventually prefer them to your existing processes, or they may inspire a new process for you.

My only word of advice regarding combining different processes is to be mindful of not over-depending on them for your wellbeing. Remember what I stressed at the beginning of this part: *you* have the power to protect yourself, not the tools you use.

# Chapter 40

# HOW TO MANAGE YOUR HEART CHAKRA AT WILL

Do you feel overwhelmed when surrounded by a large group of people? Does being in airports, train stations and concert halls make you feel anxious and uneasy? Do you avoid going out at restaurants, social gatherings and other public spaces because the energy just feels too much?

That was my experience when I first moved to London in 2014. Moving from Bristol, a much smaller city in the UK, into the hectic megacity that is London was overwhelming to say the least. Having to commute via public transport and being surrounded by hundreds of people on a daily basis was suffocating. Being an empath, I naturally picked up energy from other people and the spaces I moved through, which left me feeling drained and on-edge.

It became clear that my usual psychic protection techniques weren't enough to protect me from the immensity and intensity of the energy I was exposed to. I had to do something more.

## Managing My Heart Chakra

Consulting with my guides as to how I could manage my energy better, I was given a process to shrink and expand my aura at will. Rather than shielding my aura with layers of light that would repel psychic attack and other negative energy, shrinking my aura would limit its ability to absorb energy in the first place.

My guides also suggested that although our aura is an extension of our seven chakras, it's the heart chakra that acts as the steering wheel. Therefore, by closing and opening my heart chakra I could shrink and expand my aura, allowing me to manage by empathic sensitivity and exposure to energy.

## The End of Spiritual Martyrdom

Although having an open heart is your greatest lightworker gift, if you don't have conscious control over it, it can also be your greatest setback. Many lightworkers object to this process, suggesting that keeping their hearts open at all times is necessary for connecting deeply with people and communicating with their guides, but do you really want to connect deeply with strangers when you're on the bus heading to work in the morning? Do you consciously sit to receive guidance from your guides when you're in the supermarket or at a concert?

Being able to close and open your heart chakra at will doesn't make you less of a lightworker; the time of the spiritual martyr is over. Just because you're able to feel other people's energy and emotions doesn't mean that you have to be constantly receptive to them, or ready to jump in and save them. You can't help anyone that doesn't want or hasn't asked to be helped, and you certainly can't help those who *are* willing and ask for your help if your energy is constantly drained from all the leaks you spring for those who haven't asked for it.

Managing your heart chakra, then, is an act of self-love. It's a way for you to preserve the light you've worked so hard to nurture, so that you can work it when *you* choose in the most meaningful and effective ways.

Mastering lightwork is all about moulding and directing your light at will; it's about being aware of when it's depleted and having processes to recalibrate it; it's about knowing when you're filled up with it, and consciously channelling it to create change in the world. It's also about taking precautions to ensure that it's safe and protected from negative people and external circumstances.

## When to Close Your Heart Chakra

Before I guide you through the process of managing your heart chakra and aura at will, let's discuss the possible situations where you may need to use it.

## When you're out and about

I usually close my heart chakra when I'm going somewhere that I'll be surrounded by a large group of people that I won't need to interact or connect with much. Such places for me are airports, train stations, buses, hospitals, restaurants, public spaces (parks and busy roads), parties, clubs, cafes, the movies, the theatre, concert halls and other entertainment venues.

If I'm at any of these places with a friend or someone close to me, I only partially close my heart chakra, so that I'm able to connect with them.

## When you engage with energy vampires

Energy vampires are people with a chronically low vibrational frequency, who depend on other people for their source of happiness and positivity. Most energy vampires are easy to spot; they look depressed and unmotivated, and constantly complain about the faults of other people and the world. Others, however, camouflage themselves as cheerful and positive, as a means of getting closer to you. Once they've gained your trust, their true colours come out. They get needy and overly attached, constantly needing attention and feeding you with lies and drama.

We'll discuss ways of releasing existing emotional vampires from your life in Chapter 41, but using this process is perfect for repelling the ones that you may bump into on a daily basis.

## When to Open Your Heart Chakra

There are times when rather than closing your heart chakra, you may need to open it more than usual, therefore expanding your aura.

### *When you're hanging out with friends and family*

When you open your heart chakra and expand your aura, you're able to better connect to, empathise with and understand the people you're around. In these cases, your sensitivity to energy works to deepen your connection with the people you love. An open heart will encourage vulnerable sharing of emotions from both parties, deepening your trust and strengthening your relationships.

Being an introvert, I enjoy connecting to people one-on-one and tend to avoid large groups. This allows me to safely open my heart and aura to let the person I'm interacting with to see my authentic self. My willingness to share vulnerably gives them permission to do the same, and as we both open our hearts to each other and our auras blend, we're able to deepen our relationship.

### *When you're giving a reading, healing or consultation*

If you're a healer, an intuitive or you work in any profession that requires consulting another human being, opening your heart chakra and aura will work to your advantage. In the intuitive field specifically, opening your heart chakra before and during a session is important, as it facilitates an easier flow of intuitive communication between you and your client's higher self.

That being said, it's important to shrink your aura and cut the cords of attachment that you've established with your client immediately after the session, so that you don't get drained afterwards.

## When communicating with your guides

Expanding your aura and opening your heart chakra raises your vibration and helps you receive clear, accurate messages from your guides and inner being. I tend to open my heart chakra every morning before I start my day, so that I'm constantly open to receiving guidance from my guides. Since I spend most of my time at home, I'm not vulnerable to external negativity. Keeping my heart chakra open while I work ensures that there's a constant flow of inspiration and creativity, allowing me to perform at my best.

## Process for Expanding and Shrinking Your Heart Chakra

Follow these steps to open your heart chakra and expand your aura:

1. Get into a meditative state and focus on the beating of your heart.

2. Placing your dominant hand on your heart, visualise a golden light in the centre of it. This light is the essence of your soul. As you allow it to pour through your heart, you open your heart chakra, which prompts your aura to expand.

3. Start breathing more deeply and intently. With every breath, see the golden light within your heart growing bigger until it expands throughout your entire body.

4. Think of a happy time in your life. Go with the first happy memory that comes to mind, ideally one which instils in you the vibration of pure joy, freedom and carefreeness. These positive emotions will encourage your heart chakra and aura to expand even more.

5. As you do this, visualise your aura expanding to fill up the room you're in. When your heart chakra feels open and your aura is expanded, take some time to breathe deeply and adjust to this energy.

Follow these steps to close your heart chakra and shrink your aura:

1. Get into a meditative state and focus on the beating of your heart.

2. Placing your dominant hand on your heart, start gently tapping on your chest while breathing deeply. This is a symbolic way of asking your heart chakra to start closing and your aura to shrink.

3. Using your mind's eye, observe the state and extent of your aura enveloping your body. While tapping on your chest and breathing deeply, visualise your aura shrinking until it's only extending a few inches outside of your physical body.

4. When you're done, take some time to adjust to the new energy and come out of meditation.

# Chapter 41

# RELEASE UNHEALTHY RELATIONSHIPS

When you commit to working your light and following your life purpose, your life, your relationships and your own self will all inevitably change. You might have spent the majority of your life being disconnected from, or poorly connected to, your inner light and purpose, meaning that the lifestyle, worldview and relationships you've nurtured were all outcomes of the person you were, and so they may no longer be compatible with the person you're now becoming.

Change is never easy, especially when it comes to the human relationships you've worked so hard to nurture. Yet, resisting change and stubbornly holding on to people and relationships that no longer resonate with your newfound self will only keep you stuck in unhealthy patterns, and prevent you from following your purpose.

We spend so much time creating our relationships and so little time ending them. Ending or transitioning a relationship doesn't have to be hard or uncomfortable for you or the other person. When we take the time to end our relationships with compassion, respect and understanding, we move forward without feelings of hurt and resentment, and create the ideal emotional state to create new, healthy relationships that match the people we've become.

Not all relationships are meant to last forever. Personally, I see relationships as assignments. People come into our lives so that we can learn something together, and when we've both learned the lesson, the relationship comes to a natural end. Some relationship lessons require a lifetime or more to be fully learned, while others require a few years and others a single day.

In this chapter, I'll introduce my way of ending or transitioning three types of relationships: acquaintances, friendships and romantic partners, and family. You can use these processes as they are, or simply as inspiration to guide your own journey of releasing unhealthy relationships.

## Assess Your Relationships

Before we dive into the practical processes, it's important to get a clear idea of the quality of your current relationships. Be honest when assessing your relationships in the following exercise, observing them in an unattached and objective way.

Follow these steps to assess your current relationships:

1. List all the people you have frequent interactions with, either in person or online, under three categories: acquaintances, friendships and romantic partners, and family.

2. Once you have your list, rate each relationship on a scale of 1 to 5. A high number signifies a healthy, fulfilling relationship, while a low number signifies a draining, toxic and unfulfilling relationship.

3. Having rated your relationships, consider the reasons behind each score. If a relationship is unfulfilling, why is that? What will it take to mend or improve that relationship? Add your notes next to each name on your list.

4. Be honest with yourself. Having assessed your relationships, which of them hold you back from being fully yourself and following your life purpose? Which of these relationships would you be better off without? Which of these people are you ready and willing to release?

5. Once you've decided on the relationships that you can do without, use the cord-cutting process in Chapter 38 to release your attachment to these people.

6. Having released the energetic attachments, follow the guidelines in the next section to release them physically from your life.

## Ending vs. Transitioning Relationships

Sometimes, relationships don't have to end, but instead transition to a different kind of relationship. A close friendship may transition into an acquaintance relationship, or perhaps just a less intimate friendship. Sometimes, rather than releasing a family member from your life, you simply have to physically distance yourself from them. Not all human relationships can be dealt with in a black or white manner, and it's up to you to decide whether you want to end or transition a relationship.

Before you move on to the releasing process that follows, take some time to decide what you want to do with each of your relationships. Does the relationship have to end for you to follow your purpose fully, or simply transition?

## Guidelines for Releasing Unhealthy Relationships

It's impossible to provide step-by-step guidance as to how to end or transition relationships, because each person and relationship are different. Instead, what follows are guidelines in releasing different types of relationships based on the length and intimacy of them:

1. **Distance yourself from acquaintances.** In most cases, distancing yourself from acquaintances is enough to release the relationship. If you no longer resonate with these people during your time together, chances are they feel the same way. Therefore, when the level of intimacy is low and the period of time you've known each other is short, this mutual understanding is enough to end the relationship without any misunderstandings.

2. **Release friends and romantic partners assertively.** Things get more complicated when you have to deal with close friends or a romantic partner. Distancing yourself from them without an explanation is bound to create hurtful feelings and resentment. In this case, you have to be direct and assertive. Being assertive means stating your truth in a loving and kind way, while respecting the other person's emotions. Do this by arranging a one-on-one meeting with them, either in person, by telephone or online.

Rather than attack them, concentrate instead on explaining how *you* have changed as a person. Always end the conversation by sharing how grateful you are for everything you've experienced and gained as a result of your relationship with them.

3. **See family relationships as opportunities to grow.** In regard to family members, it is not advisable, and may not be feasible, to release them from your life completely. I strongly believe that we chose our family before we incarnated into this lifetime, in order to learn and grow together. Instead of letting them go completely, see family relationships as opportunities to love and be happy unconditionally. Of course, this doesn't apply in cases where the negativity extends to emotional or physical abuse. In those cases, the relationship has to end.

# Chapter 42

# DON'T SHARE YOUR DREAMS WITH MUGGLES

*'You're way too young to write a book. You need to have lived life first before you're ready to do so.'*

That was my dad's response when I told him that I was planning to write my first book. I was 23 years old at the time, and I was nearing the end of an eight-year journey of self-healing and self-empowerment following my almost-attempted suicide at the age of 15. I'd reverse-engineered my healing process, and I wanted to write a book that would help people find the love, acceptance and support they needed within themselves, without having to depend on others for it.

*If only he knew how much life I've already lived*, I'd thought to myself. Although I knew that my dad couldn't possibly understand where I was coming from with my desire to write a book, his rejection and lack of belief in me was still painful. At the same time, it was a blessing, as I was called to follow my book's message to stop seeking external validation, and instead find the support and encouragement that I needed within myself.

More importantly, in that moment I learned something that would be my motto with future projects and in following my life purpose: don't share your dreams with muggles.

## Interpersonal Boundaries

As lightworkers, we always see the good in people. Although we acknowledge that human nature is made up of both ego and inner being, when we look at people, we focus on their inner being. We see their light and trust in their light, forgetting that sometimes it's their ego that's taking the lead. As a result, we overshare our dreams and ourselves, and end up getting hurt or feel judged when our good intentions aren't reciprocated.

Similar to shielding our energy and establishing energetic boundaries, having interpersonal boundaries in what we share with the people in our lives is also of vital importance, regardless of how close we may be to certain people.

This is especially important when it comes to our dreams, desires and life purpose. As lightworkers in the spiritual and metaphysical communities, our dreams can often seem silly, airy-fairy and far-fetched to muggles (I use this term lovingly, to talk about people who don't share our sense of collective purpose, past life history and spiritual beliefs). Teaching about faeries, unicorns and mermaids wasn't really my parents' dream for me growing up, and had I shared my desire to study the elementals early on, they'd have probably had me institutionalised.

Additionally, due to our highly sensitive nature and our past life histories of being persecuted for our beliefs, we're often hyper-sensitive to external judgement. A single limiting comment from someone we trust and love can be detrimental to our self-esteem, and hold us back from following our purpose.

From this perspective, not sharing our dreams with muggles is an act of self-love. It's loving ourselves enough to be aware of our own sensitivity and take mindful measures to protect ourselves from comments, opinions and rejections that can discourage us.

## Don't Share Your Dreams, Period

Muggles aren't the only ones who can discourage us from following our dreams. Often, it is our fellow lightworkers whose comments can prevent us from following through with our life purpose. Even if they come from a good place, other lightworkers' opinions or cautionary tales can hinder our enthusiasm and put a cap on our action taking, holding us back from working our light.

How many times have your shared a newborn dream or desire with your spiritual friends on social media, or in real life, only to feel completely discouraged from taking action afterwards? Well-meaning, they often share their own struggle with the matter and other people's tribulations with it, or introduce a long list of tasks that need to be taken to fulfil that desire. By the end of the conversation, you feel unprepared and overwhelmed. You're convinced that you're not yet ready to follow that desire, and you end up giving up.

I've learned to keep my dreams and desires to myself until I've nurtured enough belief in them, and have taken substantial action towards them, so that nobody else's opinion can influence me. In the case of my book, following my dad's discouragement, I kept the project a secret until its publication date. I hadn't told anyone that I was writing it – not my parents, my colleagues or even my best friends. It was just my spirit guides and I throughout the entire process, until the book was published.

I still remember the day that I went to my dad holding a wrapped-up copy of my book.

*'Dad, remember two years ago, when I'd told you that I wanted to write a book? You said that I wasn't ready to do so. Well, here you go, open it'.* Flabbergasted and speechless, he unwrapped the book and stared at it, his eyes watering with pride.

Unless you feel 100% trust in your dreams and desires, and your ability to fulfil them, don't share them with other people, and that goes for muggles and lightworkers alike. Treat your dreams as newborn babies; give them the time they need to grow up and develop their personalities, so that they're able to stand on their own two feet and make it in the world without your constant care.

# CONCLUSION

Congratulations! You've made it to the end of the book. Let's take a moment to appreciate this moment. You've heard the call to follow your purpose, took action by reading this book and followed through by finishing it. You deserve a pat on the back, so go ahead and give yourself one. Be grateful for the journey you've been through.

Although our time together in this book may have come to an end, your lightworker journey never ends. Spirituality is not like a university degree; it's not something you get once and then have for the rest of your life. Spirituality is a constant, never-ending journey of choosing love over fear and keeping on doing so. It's not about being lit up 24/7, but about knowing the way to get lit up when you lose your path. It's my hope that the tools, processes and meditations in this book will help you to turn your light on when you need to.

## How to Move Forward

There are a few options for moving forward from here. If you've chosen to read the book first before applying the processes, it's time to get your journal out, choose your meditation spot and get started. Use the *Lightworkers Gotta Work Checklist* to keep track of your progress, which can be downloaded at GeorgeLizos.com/LGW

If you've been doing the processes and meditations while reading the book, here's your next plan of action:

1. **Keep updating your *Life Purpose Declaration*.** Go through the exercise of defining your life purpose every six months, amending your definition as needed. Remember that your life purpose is constantly revealing itself to you, according to your willingness and ability to accept it, and following your engagement with it. It's important to be open to your life purpose definition changing and unfolding as you grow.

2. **Prioritise your spiritual practice.** Your spiritual practice provides the fuel on your lightworker journey. If your well of light is empty, there's nothing to work with. Use the processes you've learned in the second part of the book to fill your spiritual practice with processes and activities that light you up, and be sure to make your practice a daily non-negotiable.

3. **Choose and use your favourite manifestation processes consistently.** You don't need to practice every single manifestation process I've taught you. Manifestation processes should feel good, so ensure that the processes you choose uplift you. Manifestation processes also work best when you practice them consistently, so you may want to set up 30-day manifestation challenges to manifest specific goals, or to use certain processes.

4. **Protect your energy daily, but don't obsess!** Use the psychic protection processes you've learned to clear and shield your energy on a daily basis, and keep an eye out for toxic or negative relationships that you may need to let go of. It's important to avoid obsessing over psychic protection, and instead use it as an additional protection tool in your daily practice of tuning in and lighting up. The more consistently high your vibration is, the less psychic attack you will attract.

## Less Words, More Action

I want to leave you with the same message that I started this book with:

**The world doesn't change sitting in meditation pillows all day long. The world changes when lightworkers like you and me light up and get to work.**

When we practice a bunch of spiritual and manifestation processes, it can be tempting to think that these processes *are* the action steps needed to bring our purpose into reality. In truth, the processes you've learned in this book are aimed at bringing you to the perfect state of *receiving* the action steps you need to take. Your lightwork doesn't end after setting up a manifestation altar or having finished a 30-day visualisation practice; that's when your lightwork begins!

As you practice these tools and progress on your journey, keep tuning in and reaching for the signs, impulses and guidance that must come up as a result. When the guidance comes, don't just talk, dream or bask in it, take action towards it. We spend so much time talking and dreaming about what we plan to do, and so little time taking real action towards it. So many of us are caught up in an endless cycle of wishy-washy dreaming that nurtures procrastination and keeps our purpose stuck in the ethers. We use phrases such as 'One day I *will*...' or '*When* I create this...' and then never take the action steps towards bringing these dreams into reality.

We project our happiness into the future, waiting for a divine being or a grandiose epiphany to propel us into action and create the changes we desire.

Here's the thing, lightworker: *You* are the divine being you've been waiting for, and your life purpose is the epiphany you've been asking for.

It's easy to wear the title of lightworker and share memes of inspirational quotes and crystal grids on Instagram, but unless you take action to bring your dreams, desires and purpose into the present moment, all you truly are is a light-chiller.

Instead, have the courage to see your self-sabotage for the procrastination mechanism that it is, break its stagnancy spell and take action towards your purpose. Heaven on earth isn't a utopian concept, it's a vibrational reality, and it's up to you – up to all of us – to bring it into physical manifestation.

# KEEP YOUR LIGHT ON

## Get weekly tools

Download my *Lightworker Survival Guide* to release the top-5 blocks that keep you from following your purpose. You'll also receive my weekly newsletter with more tools and guidance. Get it at georgelizos.com/lightworker-survival-guide

## Work with me

If you've enjoyed this book and want to go deeper, check out my online workshop, courses, meditations and private sessions at georgelizos.com/shop

## Get support

Meet likeminded lightworkers, enjoy guest teacher lectures and attend exclusive workshops within my private Facebook groups, *Your Spiritual Toolkit* and *Elemental Communication*.

## Feel Inspired

*The Lit Up Lightworker Podcast* features interviews with leading spiritual teachers. You'll get to fill up your spiritual toolkit with wisdom and guidance to help you follow your purpose and help in the ascension of the planet. Check it out on iTunes, Spotify, Stitcher, and TuneIn.

## Stay in touch

Tell me all about your experience with following your purpose on Instagram (@georgelizos).

# ACKNOWLEDGEMENTS

First and foremost, I'm immensely grateful to the late Atasha Fyfe, whose past-life regression in Glastonbury was the catalyst to finding my balance, and led me on the path that is the premise of this book.

To my soul sister, Emma Mildon, thank you for writing the most heartening foreword to introduce this work to the world. It's an honour to have your energy be part of the book.

Thank you, Diana Cooper, Emma Mumford, Jordan Bach, Danielle Paige, Calista, Vix Maxwell, Yasmin Boland, and Colin Bedell, for your generous endorsements and encouragement.

Thank you to the talented Ilzy Sousa for capturing the lightworker essence with her beautiful photography on the front cover.

I'm grateful to Sean Patrick for trusting me in bringing this book to life, and the amazing team at That Guy's House, Michael, Rinz, and Jo, for contributing their skills and talents.

To my friend Sargis, thank you for listening and encouraging me as I went on and on about this book.

To God Apollo, thank you for writing through me, and being a faithful companion and guide through this journey.

To Aphrodite, Hestia, Hermes, Demeter, Pan, my guides Darius, Xeros, Emanuel and Josephyl, thank you for guiding the creation and manifestation of this book.

To you, the reader, thank you for having the courage to show up for yourself, and the world.

# ABOUT THE AUTHOR

 George Lizos is a spiritual teacher, intuitive, co-creator of the *Elemental Healing™ Practitioner Course*, author of *Be the Guru* and the host of *The Lit Up Lightworker Podcast*. He helps lightworkers overcome fears and limiting beliefs that prevent them from finding and following their life purpose of finding happiness, helping others heal and creating positive change in the world.

George has been named one of the top-50 health and wellness influencers by the *Health Bloggers Community*, and his work has been featured in *Soul & Spirit*, *Kindred Spirit*, and *The Numinous*. He holds bachelor's and master's degrees in Metaphysical Sciences, a Bachelor of Science in Human Geography with a focus in Sacred Geographies, and is priest of Hellenic Polytheism.

George runs a thriving online community of empaths, lightworkers and spiritual entrepreneurs within the *Your Spiritual Toolkit* and *Elemental Communication* Facebook groups. He provides daily guidance and runs transformational workshops, aimed at overcoming the blocks that keep us stuck and prevent us from fearlessly following our purpose.

 @georgelizos

www.georgelizos.com

CPSIA information can be obtained
at www.ICGtesting.com
Printed in the USA
LVHW011741040820
662391LV00014B/1556